Researching Education

RESEARCHING EDUCATION

DATA, METHODS AND THEORY IN EDUCATIONAL ENQUIRY

David Scott and Robin Usher

CASSELL
London and New York

Cassell

Wellington House
125 Strand
London WC2R 0BB

370 Lexington Avenue
New York
NY 10017-6550

First published 1999

British Library Cataloguing-in-Publication Data
A catalogue record for this book is available from the British Library

ISBN   0-304-70459-8 (hardback)
         0-304-70460-1 (paperback)

Typeset by BookEns Ltd, Royston, Herts.
Printed and bound in Great Britain by Redwood Books, Trowbridge, Wiltshire

Contents

PART THREE: ISSUES 125

List of Figures

List of Tables

Acknowledgements

Part of Chapter 6 has previously appeared as Scott (1997). Chapters 11, 12 and 13 include material which originally appeared in Scott (1998a) and Scott (1998b) and which has been significantly revised. Permission to print this material has been granted by the London Institute of Education and Stanley Thornes (Publishers) Ltd.

ONE

Introduction

This book is a study of the theory and practice of researching education and it examines the philosophical, historical, political and social contexts of research and the implications of these for the collection and analysis of data. In doing this, it addresses such questions as: 'What is legitimate knowledge?', 'What is the relationship between the collection and analysis of data?', 'How does the researcher's presence in the field affect their data?', 'How reliable and valid are conclusions drawn from particular collections of data?' and 'How do research methods relate to epistemological and ontological debates about the nature of reality?' Above all, it seeks to problematize the practice of research and examine how power is ever-present in the construction of research texts. In a previous book (Scott and Usher, 1996: 176) we suggested that research was

> always political, although it is important to emphasise that what we mean by this is not that research is always political in a partisan sense nor indeed that it is deliberately biased and distorted so that it serves the interests of dominant groups. What we are emphasising rather is that research imposes a closure of the world through representation, it is always and inevitably involved with and implicated in the operation of power.

We suggested three other reasons for tying closely together power and knowledge: research always takes place within settings whose structuring depends on micro-political processes; since in education there is no single correct research procedure and no superordinate methodology, power relations feature in and between research traditions; and social research is always valued research, in that both the values of participants in the research and the values of the researcher themselves are central to the construction of research texts.

In opposition to this, educational research is frequently understood in the following way:

- Nomothetic statements about educational activities, structures and systems are possible.
- Educational disputes can be settled by empirical enquiry.
- The values, preconceptions and epistemological frameworks of the researcher are irrelevant to the design of the research, and are certainly not reported in the research text.
- It is possible to develop theory about education which is superior to practical knowledge. Practice is therefore understood as the efficient application of theoretical knowledge which has been constructed by professional researchers.
- There is a correct method for collecting educational data. If this is not followed, then conclusions drawn from the data may be unsound.

In this book we suggest, through close examination of the various issues surrounding research, that this viewpoint neglects, indeed acts to conceal, those epistemological and ontological relations that underpin all types of research activity. What this implies is that power is central to the research act and we simply cannot dismiss it from our epistemological endeavours, but must try to understand its effects. This involves a reflexive understanding of the way in which we are positioned as knowers, and it suggests that the scientific paradigm of a singular, convergent and fragmentable reality which can be known by researchers who act independently from the subjects of their research and who produce generalizations and nomothetic statements is not sustainable.

Part One of the book examines the philosophical context of educational research. We begin by problematizing the idea of research as a 'technology', a set of methods, skills and procedures to be implemented. Research is understood as a social practice, in which relations of power are ever-present. This is contrasted with positivist/empiricist research, which may be understood as having the following characteristics: determinacy (there is a certain truth that can be known); rationality (there are no contradictory explanations); impersonality (the more objective and the less subjective the better); and prediction (research is the making of knowledge claims in the form of generalizations from which predictions can be made, and events and phenomena controlled). This has been criticized for offering a false picture of reality and how we can know it, certainly in the social sciences and possibly in the natural sciences as well. Kuhn (1970), for instance, argues that: data and observation are theory-led; theory is located in paradigms; and those paradigms are historically and culturally specific.

Three alternatives are suggested in this book. The first of these is interpretivism. Here the emphasis is on human action, and the assumption is made that it is meaningful and hence has to be interpreted and understood. The philosophical tradition of phenomenology from its earliest surfacings in the writings of Edmund Husserl (1960) to the later mature hermeneutics of Hans-Georg Gadamer (1975) exemplifies this. The second alternative has come to be known as the critical theory tradition, the leading proponent of which is Jurgen Habermas (1987). Critical theory is 'critical' in the sense that it challenges both the positivist/empiricist and hermeneutic/interpretive traditions of social research, and refers to the detecting and unmasking of beliefs and practices that limit human freedom. The third alternative is post-positivism or postmodernism. Proponents of these argue that research, even 'scientific' research, is a product of certain kinds of social, historically located, practices. Post-positivism reflects a distrust of absolutes and foundational truths. No longer does following the correct method guarantee true results. Instead of only one truth, there are many. As will have become obvious from this brief discussion, we are suggesting that the research process cannot be properly understood without addressing epistemological and ontological questions. Indeed, this is our starting point. Most educational research either denies the relevance of these questions or deems it unnecessary to surface those ontological and epistemological relations which underpin the collection of data about activities, institutions and systems.

Chapter 4 provides an account of the four research strategies commonly used by educational researchers: induction, deduction, retroduction and abduction. The first of these, where theory-building always proceeds from the collection of observable facts, has been criticized on two grounds: data can never be free of the preconceptions and frameworks of the data collector, and any theory developed may be falsified by new facts which come to light. The deductive approach has been criticized because it fails to take account of those mechanisms which drive events and activities but which may not be reflected in the constant conjunction of observable events. Retroduction in turn has been criticized for a belief in realism, albeit of a sophisticated kind, which, moreover, includes the existence of unobservable entities. Abductive researchers argue that we can only know social reality through the eyes of the social actors involved in it. There is a weak and a strong version. In the first case, researchers should never go beyond the constructs used by participants; in the second, though observer constructs should be anchored in lay concepts, it is legitimate for the researcher to use constructs which lay actors do not initially recognize.

Part Two examines the different methods used by educational researchers, always mindful that a method is used in a particular way and for a particular purpose, and this orientation is always buttressed by wider concerns. We begin with an exploration of the experimental method as it is used in educational and social research. As with all the different approaches discussed in this book, we offer a sustained critique. We argue that the experimental method is deficient for five reasons. The first of these is that the effects of interventions may be more subtle or difficult to conceptualize than experimentalists allow for. Furthermore, the method may be inappropriate for examining those causal mechanisms which underpin social life, because experimentalists adopt a 'successionist' rather than a 'generative' theory of causation. They also make the assumption that the context of human relations is not central to an understanding of it and that the way in which social actors understand their lives is not an essential part of the research process. Experimentalists fail to adequately solve the problem of ecological validity, which is that since they construct artificial settings for examining human behaviour, they cannot then be certain that other human beings will behave like this in real life. Finally, there are ethical problems with experimentation because the method is discriminatory, even if it is not known until the end of the experiment who is being discriminated against.

The second major approach discussed in Part Two is survey and correlational research. Survey researchers attempt to collect data about larger populations than are usual with experimental or case study research. Chapter 6 details the various survey methods, highlighting, in particular, their concentration on the variable and the need for quantification. In it we discuss a number of criticisms that have been made: survey researchers are not responsive to what is being researched; they pre-specify which data are to be collected and in what way; and they reduce complicated human activity to data sets expressed in numerical terms. The method also makes claims which are consistent with a positivist/empiricist approach to research, e.g. that it is possible to develop a science of educational research and that this science comprises the making of nomothetic statements about educational activities. These claims are discussed in the last part of this chapter.

Traditionally, some methodological strategies (experimental, single-case, ex-post facto, correlational and survey) have been designated as quantitative, and others (ethnography and condensed case study) as qualitative. More recently, various attempts have been made to sublate the divide between the two types of strategies and sets of methods. However, we argue in Chapter 7 that there are two compelling reasons for distinguishing between them. The first is to do with the thought idiom that structures research. Mathematical modellers are not able to deal with the intentions, beliefs and propositional attitudes of social actors. If they try to, they are engaged in processes of reification, packaging and ultimately distortion. This implies that data-collection processes which do not involve quantification have to be employed to fully understand the nature of the social world. The second argument is more complicated. It suggests that there is a necessary relationship between the four levels at which researchers operate – method, strategy, epistemology and ontology – and that the quantitative–qualitative distinction can be shown to be inappropriate when applied at the first two levels, but to be significant at the levels of epistemology and ontology.

The next three chapters each take a commonly used research method and discuss those epistemological and ontological relations which underpin particular uses. Chapter 8 examines four observer field roles: complete participant, participant as observer, observer as participant and complete observer. In addition, we argue that the degree and type of structure used by observers is central to an understanding of this method. In a similar way, researchers may use different types of interviews and these can be distinguished by their different types of structure. Chapter 10 explores biographical and autobiographical methods, in particular where life-history researchers adopt intensive interview techniques to explore the lives and careers of teachers and other educational workers.

Part Three examines a number of issues which are central to the research process. In Chapter 11 we discuss the various ethical approaches adopted by empirical researchers: covert, open democratic and open autocratic; the epistemological frameworks which underpin these approaches; and the relationship between these ethical approaches and the types of data collected. Chapter 12 extends this discussion and at the same time unpicks the distinction which is commonly made between evaluation and research. It further explores the theory and practice of evaluation as it has come to be understood and practised over the past thirty years in different institutional, local and national policy contexts. In Chapter 13 we look at whether it is possible to develop sets of criteria to judge educational research. Positivist–empiricist researchers argue that research involves representation of an independent reality, neutrality, the use of asituational and atemporal observational techniques, a notion of linear causality and the possibility of objective inquiry. Hermeneutical researchers, critical theorists and postmodernists reject such criteria. Chapter 14 examines a possible alternative: transgressive research.

The argument in this book moves from a discussion of philosophical relations to the more prosaic – the actual practice of research. This mirrors our thinking, in that surfacing the epistemological and ontological assumptions of research strategies and methods is frequently neglected. Furthermore, this neglect means that the practice of research is undertheorized and it therefore acts to deny its readers the means by which they can make proper judgements about its worth.

PART ONE

Philosophy

TWO

The Place of Philosophical Issues in Educational Research

Philosophical issues tend not to occupy a prominent place in books on educational research. This is partly to do with the close links between educational research and educational practice, which has tended to foreground the 'doing' of the former and its application to the latter rather than a consideration of the philosophical assumptions and issues with which the 'doing' is entangled. An emphasis on the 'doing' of research inevitably means an emphasis on methods and procedures, since these are in a sense the most obvious manifestations of the 'doing'. Being 'concealed' in the research process, they seem to be speculative and abstruse and, to a large extent, apparently unnecessary in relation to the immediate practical task of getting research going and bringing it to a successful outcome. There seems, therefore, to be no pressing need to integrate them into the research process itself. However, another reason why philosophical and in particular epistemological issues are concealed is related to the power of positivism and its associated realist metaphysics. Even when researchers are not conscious of working within the general parameters of positivism, the latter still exerts a powerful influence – an influence which considers reflexive questions to be both undesirable and unnecessary. We will consider the nature and influence of positivism and realism more fully later. For the moment, however, we can say that, whatever its source, this quality of concealment means that the place and significance of philosophical issues only becomes apparent 'after the event' of research and generally in the process of critiques such as this.

In this book, however, we will, without neglecting proper consideration of methods and procedures, try to reverse the disprivileging of philosophical issues and bring them more to the forefront of, and by this means recognize their central place in, the research process. We will in fact assume that philosophical issues are *integral* to the research process and cannot be ignored until after the event. We will argue that this is so because philosophical issues constitute what researchers 'silently think' about research. The contemporary situation is such that we now need to think loudly and publicly, not just about methods, outcomes and applications, but about the research process itself; and to think in this way not after the event but during it.

What is it, then, that we silently think when it comes to research? Obviously, this is a question which does not readily lend itself to a single answer. One possible answer is to do with the tendency to assume that doing research is simply a matter of following the right procedures or methods. This assumption, however, needs to be questioned because it misleadingly portrays research as mechanistic and algorithmic. If we uncritically accept this portrayal we forget that research is a social practice and that it is therefore both embedded and embodied. Thus one thing we can do in terms of becoming more aware of what we silently think is to recognize that research is not a technology but a practice, that it is not individualistic but social and that there are no universal methods to be applied invariantly.

Another possible answer to the question of what we silently think about research is to do with the powerful binary opposition 'quantitative–qualitative' and its privileging of the former over the latter, with the implication that quantitative research is 'better' in the sense of being more *legitimate* as research. It is not so long ago that qualitative research tended to be totally discounted as 'soft', unrigorous and subjective, with researchers always having to justify their 'unconventional' methodology and having to work hard to 'prove' the validity of their outcomes. Of course, this situation is now not so prevalent; qualitative research has become more accepted, and with this the argument has tended to shift from the legitimacy of qualitative research to its compatibility with quantitative research, given their apparently radically divergent assumptions about the nature of knowledge.

However, this is not to say that the continuing struggle to get qualitative research fully legitimated no longer takes place. This struggle is not so acute within the field of education itself, since it is fought more between the 'hard' and 'soft' disciplines of the social sciences, with education usually lining up with the latter and the former calling on the 'ultra-hard' natural sciences for support. Whilst, therefore, this is obviously still an important struggle for educational researchers, they are also very much aware that qualitative research is itself not unproblematic – in many ways, it has as many problematic features as quantitative research, with many of these being surprisingly similar. At the same time, there is reason to suppose that educational researchers might be rather bored by these debates. Many of the problematic elements arise precisely because of the search for legitimacy, and increasingly many are beginning to question whether legitimacy is that important anyway. This takes us back to the compatibility issue. Whether or not qualitative and quantitative methods are compatible, the very foregrounding of issues of compatibility functions to maintain 'legitimacy' within its own self-defined terms, terms which have provided the reference points or 'rules of the game' for *all* research approaches.

The debate now is whether rather than continuing the somewhat pointless conflict about what is legitimate and what is not, maybe we should problematize the very desire for legitimacy; in doing this we might well come to recognize that what is most needed is a space for scrutinizing the assumptions that shape the meaning of research itself, whether it be quantitative or qualitative. Increasingly, many are asking whether we need to think about ways in which the whole enterprise of research can be reconceptualized or reconfigured. However, reconfiguring research is no easy task, and questions of legitimacy cannot simply be made to vanish. To understand why this is the case requires a consideration of mostly neglected epistemological issues, and it is such a consideration which is vital in uncovering what we silently think about research.

Epistemology has traditionally been concerned with what distinguishes different knowledge claims – specifically with what the criteria are that allow distinctions to be made between what is legitimately knowledge and what is simply opinion or belief. Epistemology is supposed to answer the question: how do we know what we think we know? Historically, it is an aspect of the Enlightenment's dismantling of tradition and experience as sources of knowledge. With this dismantling came the question of how any knowledge claim could be considered valid or indeed how it was possible to 'know' anything. What epistemology was essentially seen as doing was creating a set of rules for knowing by drawing boundaries and setting up mechanisms to police those boundaries. By application of the rules, only certain kinds of knowledge would be considered valid; the rest would be refused that status. Very quickly, the rules or grounds for this validity came to be found in scientific method in the form of measurement, in testability and in the use of reason. Through empiricism, sense experience (rather than life experience) gained through observation and experiment became the 'given', the source or grounding of knowledge. Epistemological issues came to be seen purely in empiricist terms, with science as the privileged model of investigation.

Now, any research, whether in the natural or social sciences, makes knowledge claims and for that reason alone is implicated in epistemological questions. Indeed, it could be argued that all research has an underlying epistemology, even though this is rarely made explicit. As we have noted, most of the time the epistemology is either unrecognized or taken for granted. It is simply assumed that the research will be positivist–empiricist in its epistemology and therefore unproblematic: hence the power of quantitative methods most obviously located within its parameters. Nowadays, this taken-for-granted approach to epistemology is no longer considered adequate. Thus, for example, making a knowledge claim is not just a matter of appealing to universal rules of validity, since claims are justified within collectively held conceptions about the world and how to relate to it; in other words, as we have argued earlier, producing knowledge claims is a social practice. It is the social conceptions that are embodied in an epistemology, the most powerful of which is the conception that holds up the methods and procedures of the natural sciences as the model for producing valid knowledge claims. Thus the 'rules' for policing knowledge claims are themselves culturally located; epistemologies thus become as much as about politics or power as they are about logic.

Positivism is an epistemological position which affirms the facticity of the world. It argues that, since the only possible content of true statements is facts, it is scientific method that reveals facts about the world. Scientific method is the set of rules which guarantee accurate representation – a correspondence between what reality is and how it is represented in knowledge. There are fundamental laws expressible as universal generalizations governing both the natural and social worlds and discoverable through scientific activity. Positivism therefore equates legitimacy with science (albeit an idealized picture of science) and scientific method (in the sense of a set of general methodological rules). All this involves a number of assumptions. One is that the world is 'objective' in the sense that it exists independently of those who seek to know it. Thus there is a clear distinction or separation to be made between subjects (knowers) and objects (the world). Facts are to do with the world and are therefore 'objective', whereas values and concerns are to do with the 'subjective', which must not be allowed to interfere with the process of discovering facts. Second, assertions about the world and hence the validity of knowledge claims are about observable measurable phenomena. Furthermore, different observers, given their possession in common of a reasoning faculty should come to the same conclusions about what they observe. Third, the social world is not essentially different from the natural world. There are order and reason, patterns and cause–effect forms in the former just as in the latter. It follows from this that all the sciences share a common logic and method of enquiry.

Although these assumptions are significant and need to be problematized, their very foregrounding can convey the impression that positivism is simply an abstruse epistemological doctrine without much purchase in the 'real world' of day-to-day research. This, however, is misleading, since positivism defines not only a way of doing research but also a way of theorizing social reality – a way that has massive social consequences. As a way of doing research it involves accepting the position that there is a set of logical rules of explanation, independent of the world and its social practices, which can distinguish between and judge all knowledge claims. It involves accepting that research is a matter of observation and measurement, that it has a universal rather than an embedded rationality and that it works with a unitary and invariant set of methods.

However, the most significant thing about positivism for our purposes is that it is not simply an epistemology but more importantly a way of theorizing social reality. Positivism is a continuation of the grand narrative of the Enlightenment that only a society based on science and its universal values can be rational and therefore truly free. This is a narrative of cultural progress where modernity is depicted as a process of science replacing not only religion and tradition but also practical wisdom and experience as the foundation of social organization, and where the law-like generalizations of science form the basis of expertise (developed through research) that informs and justifies policy- and decision-making.

The contemporary world, is of course, characterized by the intimate connections between research, expertise and policy-making. As Gitlin and Russell (1994) point out, educational researchers are considered experts because of their research-based knowledge and are distinguishable from those who are to be informed by that knowledge. This is simply another facet of the theory–practice binary, with the former privileged over the latter, a binary which has caused many problems in both educational practice and research. It is positivism which shapes this position and technical-rationality, the enactment of positivist principles in the realm of practice, which plays a key role. Technical-rationality involves practices of expertise based on the law-like generalizations or nomothetic statements based on scientifically derived knowledge. It is the deployment of instrumental rationality in choosing the most efficient means based on expertise in achieving pre-specified ends. With technical-rationality there is an assumption that ends are outside the sphere of rationality, since ends are matters of value rather than fact, and values, for the positivist, are not factual. As Parker (1997) points out, the 'characters' in this narrative are the detached academic researcher, the expert professional, the manager, the bureaucrat and the inspector.

However, there are many who would argue that there are few who nowadays believe in positivism. There is much truth in this argument, since positivism has undoubtedly been subjected to a great deal of hard critique, probably to the extent where few would wish to support it purely as an epistemological position. Yet it would be a serious mistake to therefore think of positivism simply as a philosophical curiosity, fit only for the dustbin of history. It could be argued, on the contrary, that this is far from being the case, since it still remains a dominant philosophy in practice, and of course is particularly alive and well in the practices of technical-rationality, itself still influential in educational research, practice and policy-making.

To understand why this is the case it is also necessary to recognize that positivism and technical-rationality are themselves not the whole story. Another layer is provided by the conceptual framework of *realism*, a framework that is presupposed by positivism and the practices of technical-rationality. Whilst philosophically there are many variants of realism, there are certain common features. The best known variant could be characterized simply as common sense expressed in philosophical language, which is perhaps what makes it so powerful yet at the same time masked in its effects. Our common-sense intuition tells us that the world exists independently of our lives and sociocultural practices, including the practice of research. We feel that the world is 'real', that it exists around us 'out there', indifferent to our hopes, beliefs and desires at any particular moment. This independent, 'objective' world is the yardstick against which we must measure our hopes, beliefs, etc. in order to assess and establish their truth and reality. The nature of the world out there is something about which we can make discoveries through research, and our knowledge increases with every discovery. Thus research in the scientific mode brings us closer to true descriptions of the world in the form of theories that express these truths. Realism overlaid by positivism can thus be summed up in three propositions – first, that reality is self-evidently available; second, that science is free of its own cultural confusions; and third, that knowledge is produced by means of immutable methods (Lemert, 1997).

The independent existence of the world is the essence of the view of objectivity shared by common sense, science and technical-rationality. Truth is achieved through applying appropriate rationally grounded techniques – hence the notion of research as a technical process that we pointed to earlier. Once a statement about the world is found to be true, it is true absolutely for everyone anywhere. For any field of understanding, there will be one true description of the world, and this description must command universal assent, since once a truth is established it is unassailable; it has a cognitive authority which makes it irrational not to assent to it. Moreover, the values 'true' or 'false' as applied to statements about the world exhaust all possibilities. One cannot have 'true just for x' or 'neither true nor false' – realism inclines us to believe that such statements would literally be meaningless. All propositional statements must be either true or false, and must be non-contradictory, since otherwise no true description of the world would be possible, given the consequent plurality of incommensurable truths.

In realism, the relation between theories that explain the world and the world itself has to be understood on the model of the external perspective, the God's-eye point of view. One comes to know about the world but without being in it. The world consists of independently existing objects of which there can only be one *true* description – a description that is guaranteed by the elimination of researcher bias and the ambiguity of language. Truth is a matter of *correspondence* between statements about the world contained in theories and the way the world is, its reality. It is the *presence* of reality, therefore, that determines truth, that is in effect the measure of truth – presence is the 'voice' of nature, the origin, the authorizing centre, which places the necessary restrictions or limits on how the world can be described, and how it can be known. It eliminates any distortion in representing or knowing the world so that the latter can be represented in the language of knowledge. The priority or pre-existence of the world 'as it really is' over any descriptions we make of it implies that the role of language is to be a transparent medium that enables the world to be accurately represented. Language is tied to the world through relations of correspondence between names and sentences and objects and states of the world. Thus for the realist the only language that counts is language which is referential and literal, with pure and unambiguous meanings, free from the distortions of interpretation and the figural.

Embodied in realism is a picture of a universally correct standard of rationality operating according to the laws of inferential logic. Individuals are considered to be endowed with the capacity, although to varying degrees, of exercising this rationality – a rationality that is thus seen as an essence of a natural kind rather than an outcome and function of the norms and practices of particular societies. Knowledge can be systematically extended by deploying this invariant and universal standard of rationality. For realism, therefore, the history of science is that of a cumulative, linear progression from ignorance to knowledge, a steady and inexorable movement away from incompleteness and error. Here, then, we have clearly presented a manifestation of Enlightenment thought, a suitable metaphysics of and for modernity. Whilst there are other and more sophisticated variants of realism (such as critical realism, which will be discussed in more detail later), there is none the less a common theme running throughout all these variants. Critical theorists, for example, accept that the world is only known through particular descriptions, so facts are not simply waiting around to be discovered. They agree that knowledge is a social and historical product but they also argue that certain kinds of knowledge (or 'best' descriptions) can accurately represent the world. Thus they refuse to accept that there can be more than one best description or many knowledges. They also believe that it is possible to develop rational criteria that are not context-dependent. But as Scheurich (1997) points out, not only are there insuperable difficulties in defining these criteria and deciding which of them to give most weight to in choosing between theories, but there is also the problem that the criteria themselves have no empirical or rational foundation. Hence they can only be historically relative, particular to particular disciplinary contexts.

Earlier, we mentioned that positivism has been subjected to a hard critique. In particular, notions such as the immutability of methods and the linear cumulative progress of scientific knowledge were dealt a severe blow by Kuhn (1970). He argued that scientific discovery belongs to the realm of the cultural and the historical rather than the transcendental. The powerful realist picture we have of scientific research is essentially philosophical, a projection of a particularly Western understanding and history. Furthermore, there is a divergence between the avowed methodology and self-understandings of scientists and their actual practice. Kuhn focused instead on science as an activity and by doing so showed that scientific understanding consisted not only of theories and laws but also of metaphysical commitments such as realism, which are 'taught' through the doing of scientific research. His work has stimulated the post-positivist critique of scientific research and of positivism's idealized and ahistorical reconstruction of science. Post-positivism foregrounds the actual practices of science and by looking at the historical development of a variety of scientific knowledges, puts forward an anti-essentialist position on knowledge, one that focuses on the local and situational features of scientific practices, and which denies any single and universal set of features qualifying a practice as scientific.

The post-positivist critique has provided a means of arguing that the realist–positivist view of science is oppressive, limiting and possibly even untenable. But again we cannot extrapolate from this and argue that realism is dead. Indeed, one could argue quite the opposite – that realism is still pervasive, despite the inroads of post-positivism, and has stubbornly refused to succumb to the onslaught of this critique. Part of the reason for this is, as Stuart Parker (1997: 21) points out, that it is a *metaphysical* framework which actually goes *beyond* common sense but does so in an unnoticed way: 'so omnipresent, so innocuous, are the assumptions it embodies and so seemingly inevitable ... its implications.' How obvious it seems, for example, that the world exists independently of us; how obvious that the measure of truth should be its correspondence with reality; how obvious that we should be able to delimit knowledge and separate the valid from the invalid; and how obvious, given the success of science, that scientific method should be the guarantee of validity and the road to truth. And as Foucault (1980) has pointed out, who, after all, can argue with 'truth'? It is significant here how Parker's point is supported, in that with each one of these statements we progressively move further away from common-sense intuition into realism as a metaphysical thesis that goes far beyond such intuition.

We can see this metaphysics most clearly articulated in quantitative research and more generally in the empirical–analytic research paradigm. Yet more controversially, it could be argued that it is also present in other research paradigms that are apparently different. Not in an obvious way perhaps, and certainly with the more extreme positivistic features removed, along with the applied practice of technical-rationality; yet there none the less. It is this which perhaps accounts for some of the problematic elements in qualitatively oriented paradigms – strange though this may seem at first sight. Some of these problematic areas are by now well known. To explain what we mean by this we need to be aware that most research, regardless of its locating paradigm, tends to manifest a refusal to question how researchers create their texts. Political stances are seen as simply evaporating; in other words, there is an assumption that researchers can free themselves of their own cultural confusions. That researchers invent some questions and repress others, that they shape the contexts they study, that they are co-participants in interviews, that they interpret other's stories and narrate their own, is all considered to be irrelevant. In other words, texts are created that are author(itative) but seemingly without author(ity). Such texts obscure the ways in which researchers *construct* their analyses and narratives – they are written as if researchers were simply vehicles for transmission with no voice of their own. Yet this stance is nothing to do with the world or the nature of its objective reality (as realism would have it) but everything to do with *textuality*, with the rhetorical devices and conventions that organize meanings in the research text in particular ways and for particular effects – a stance that realism necessarily cannot accept.

It was Donna Haraway (1991) who most aptly caricatured this epistemological fetish with detachment and neutrality when she described the 'God trick ... [as] that mode of seeing that pretends to offer a vision that is simultaneously from everywhere and nowhere, equally and fully' (Haraway, 1991: 584); a narrative of universal truth that at the same time denies the 'truth' of the privileges, interests and politics of researchers. This is the so-called 'objectivity' of researchers that we mentioned earlier, an 'objectivity' that casts researchers as abstracted individuals without specificity – interchangeable knowers possessed only of the faculty of reason. As well as the textuality of research, what are foregrounded in this way are issues to do with power. There is an appropriate colonial analogy here, since the relationship between researcher and subjects can be likened to that of colonist and subjects. It is the former who defines the problem, the nature of the research, the quality of the interaction between researcher and researched, the theoretical framework and the categories of analysis; and, of course, who writes the final text. Researchers (whether quantitative or qualitative) are essentially in the business of creating coherent narratives, narratives that are 'masterful' and that require the Other for their coherence, but where these constructions of the Other tend 'towards a strategy of containment where the Other is forever the exegetical horizon of difference, never the active agent of articulation' (Bhabha, 1994: 31).

Michelle Fine (1994), a leading feminist researcher, argues that all researchers are epistemic agents, both embodied and embedded, who choose political and epistemological stances. She characterizes the denial of this in the stance of neutrality and objectivity as 'ventriloquy', a stance that relies upon Haraway's 'God trick'. She argues that ventriloquy means never having to say 'I' in the text, it means treating subjects as objects while calling them subjects, and it requires the denial of all politics in the inevitably political work of doing research. However, Fine also describes an alternative stance of 'voices' that is located in an interpretive research paradigm which, on the face of it, seems to avoid these problems but which, on closer examination, itself proves problematic. What are again illustrated here are issues of power, textuality and the place of the researcher but with a different configuration of the problems. Fine argues that 'voices' offers a tremendous opportunity for researchers interested in generating critical, counter-hegemonic analyses of institutional arrangements. However, although these voices may contain critical insights, they are embedded in the scripts of dominant groups. Thus a romantic reliance on these voices – as though they were simply innocent words of critique – can amount to a more sophisticated form of ventriloquy, thus reinstating it through the back door. Here, whilst the Other is allowed to speak, and presumably through speaking supposedly becomes empowered, the researcher hides under the cover of those 'empowered' voices whilst doing the empowering.

These voices are not just raw data – they are not simply unequivocal voices of critique. Rather, what they show is that subjects are multiply situated; their perspectives are full of social contradictions, and their experiences are not easily captured within the familiar categories of social science. Therefore, these experiences cannot simply be taken at face value, since they are not events *per se* but reconstructed stories. To simply transcribe experiences is to fail to examine critically constructions which are very 'real' to informants – yet which require criti-cal examination because they are so real. To take 'unadulterated' voices as givens, as a presence, an authorizing centre, as valid because they are 'unadulterated voices', is to forget that any voice is *both an interpretation and itself in need of interpretation*. Of course, it is vital not to be imperialistic about this, but the refusal to be critical pans out as 'either a form of condescension or a hyper-protocol reserved only for Others with whom serious intellectual work is inappropriate' (Fine, 1994: 21). Most significantly, this refusal is located in the realist metaphysic of objectivity, presence and transparency – that the world exists independently of the knower, ready to be known in an unmediated way.

The methodological implication of this is that, along with any ethnographic rendition of voices, the researcher has *to consciously* reinsert an interpretive self (the stress here is deliberate because this self is usually concealed). To critique 'voices' as a stance that orients a way of doing research is not to deny the legitimacy of qualitative data such as interview material. But it does remind us that when research texts are organized in terms of voices construed as isolated and innocent moments of experience, this is often an excuse for researchers not to explicate their own stances and their relations with their subjects. It also reminds us that even in the most 'empowering' research, issues of power are never absent. Indeed, they are always already present, inscribed in the text regardless of intent or locating paradigm.

We are not arguing that different research paradigms and traditions, e.g. empirical–analytic and interpretive, are all the same – more or less overt versions of positivism. What we are trying to point to, however, is the realist metaphysic of unmediated access to the world and the hope of faithful representation of the world, which is present in all in some form. It is this representational problem located in the general problematic of research's capture by realism that critical ethnography has tried to address. Again, we are not arguing that critical ethnography is the only approach that has resolved the problems raised by realism – what we are saying is that critical ethnography is an example of a contemporary approach that attempts to address these problems by foregrounding the textuality of research and the place of writing, in the broadest sense, within the research process.

To quote James Clifford, a leading critical ethnographer:

> we begin not with methods but with writing ... no longer a marginal or occulted dimension, writing has emerged as central to what researchers do both in the field and thereafter ... the fact that it has not until recently been portrayed or seriously discussed reflects the persistence of an ideology claiming transparency of representation and immediacy of experience. (Clifford and Marcus, 1986: 2)

Clifford goes on to argue that science is in, not above, historical and linguistic processes – an argument similar to Lyotard's (1984) that scientific knowledge is always a kind of discourse – with the implication that it is impossible for science to free itself of its cultural location and hence of its own cultural confusions. The focus on writing, text-making and rhetoric highlights the constructed and *contested* nature of cultural accounts (which it could be argued is what research in all its different guises basically is). It undermines transparent modes of authority and draws attention to the fact that ethnography, for example, is not about representing the world but about 'inventing' or 'fictioning' it, or, to put it another way, 're-presenting' it. As with Geertz's (1973) account of the Balinese cock-fight (which Clifford, amongst others, has critiqued), there is only 'the constructed understanding of the constructed native's constructed point of view' (Crapanzano, 1986: 74).

In fact, Geertz's detailed interpretation of the betting at a Balinese cock-fight is worth pursuing a little further at this point. According to Bohman (1991), Geertz's interpretation constructs the cock-fight as a social text that can be read and understood. In seeing it this way, he is textually and rhetorically creating the conditions for analysing the cock-fight as an object of interpretation, the problem being that, because of cross-cultural distance, the sense the cock-fight has for the Westerner is not the same as it has for the Balinese. Clifford's critique is a direct challenge to the assumed authority of the ethnographic interpreter. It may well be the case that what is going on for the Balinese is different from what is going on for the Western ethnographer, but at the same time it is undoubtedly the case that a Balinese phenomenon is being explained in Western terms. It is not a matter of whether Geertz is right or wrong, whether his explanation is true or false, since what is at stake here is a way of seeing and the power intrinsic to that. Geertz's interpretation of the cock-fight as an artform is still ethnocentric, a Western way of understanding, despite the 'thick description' of context.

This constructed understanding of the constructed native's point of view is, in an important sense, a 'fiction', not because it is untrue but because Geertz's interpretation is one of many possible truths. What this points to is that although research is generally thought of as a process of 'finding out' about the world, there is also a need to take account of the reflexive dimension in research. Reflexivity is about 'finding out' how meanings, including the meanings given to and generated by research, are discursively constructed within the research process. One implication of foregrounding reflexivity and discursive construction is the recognition that academic and literary genres interpenetrate, and this itself has implications for epistemological questions of validity. Given the embeddedness of realism in Western science, there has always been a rigorous exclusion (in the name of rigour) of expressive modes, e.g. rhetoric in favour of plain, transparent signification; fiction in favour of fact; subjectivity in favour of objectivity. These expressive modes have been consigned to 'literature', and so literature becomes the feared and rejected 'other' of science which is always necessary to establish the credibility and very being of scientific research. Literary texts were deemed to be metaphorical and allegorical, expressing inventions rather than observed facts and privileging multiple effects of meaning rather than singular meaning. Above all, they violated referential language and the principal of bivalence, narrating one thing in order to say something else, often of a contradictory nature.

Yet the literary dimension is not so easy to mark off-limits and out of bounds by this construction of otherness, since literary processes – metaphor, figuration, narrative, expressive tropes generally – that select and impose meaning as they translate it, all, as Clifford points out, affect the way in which phenomena are registered, encoded or inscribed, from the first fieldwork jottings to the completed text and to the way in which sense is made through acts of reading. But these literary processes, endemic in all forms of research, yet concealed by realist metaphysics, not only highlight the rhetorical nature of research but also function as devices making possible systematic exclusions that enable the very possibility of 'truth'. Thus what we have here is yet another hierarchical binary opposition (scientific research–literature) which, when deconstructed, shows the interdependence of the two terms rather than their opposition. The deconstruction of this binary opposition implies, therefore, that research texts do not simply report 'truth'. They are not simply a written record of what went on in the research process and what was found out about the world. Rather, they are implicated in *economies* of truth; for example, Geertz's research is implicated in the ethnocentric economy of truth of Western ethnography.

At this point, having mentioned 'writing', it might be appropriate to say something more about the notion of 'text' – a notion that is extraordinarily controversial and yet is critical in thinking of ways in which research might be thought of differently. A starting point might be Roland Barthes' words from *The Semiotic Challenge* (1975: 308) – 'the text . . . is fundamentally to be distinguished from the literary work . . . it is not an aesthetic product, it is a signifying practice'. He argues that to talk in terms of 'text', and to conceive of 'text' as a signifying practice, implies that the practice of 'science', or indeed the practice generally of generating bodies of validated knowledge, must question its own discourse – or to put it another way, recognize its own cultural confusions by being reflexive. Furthermore, the responsibility of any practice that questions itself is that it cannot just challenge positivism and simply locate itself as post-positivist but must take responsibility for itself. It must be *political* in the sense that it recognizes its own implication with power and accepts the moral dimension that is intrinsic in interpreting the utterances and actions of others.

One obvious thing that gets in the way of understanding the significance of 'text' in the research process is the tendency to understand the term literally as nothing more than a particular piece of writing. But beyond this, what also gets in the way of understanding is the substitution of methodology for text. Again, it could be argued that this is an outcome of a failure to problematize realism, since the realist metaphysic has accustomed us to privileging methodology. Our 'intuition' is to see it as something whose proper use will guarantee better accounts and above all provide the necessary certainty about the validity of research outcomes. But the foregrounding of textuality now makes this uncertain. By thinking in terms of text rather than methodology we might be more inclined to consider the *necessary* failure of the certainty that has been methodology's hope – particularly now that the realist dream of finding an innocent and transparent language that will faithfully represent 'reality' has been so thoroughly challenged, or, perhaps, one could say now that it has been deconstructed through the notion of text and 'discourse'.

At the same time, however, whilst we may no longer be quite so concerned to look for grounds of certainty, we do not seem to have any fully worked out alternative – certainly text and discourse are not (and indeed probably cannot be) an alternative in this sense. But at the same time, we cannot just passively accept the notion that to escape from the crisis of representation is therefore impossible. If that were the case then we would have to stop doing research altogether, for research must inevitably involve representation. Stronach and MacLure (1997) suggest that one possibility is to think in terms of research which strategically interrupts (and disrupts) rather than accepts or rejects totally the methodological will to clarity and certainty. Such interruptions and disruptions would breach the epistemological boundaries delineating and protecting domains of expert knowledge, taking apart master discourses and policy texts to expose the power–knowledge formations inscribed therein.

In conceiving of this possibility, the work of Patti Lather (1986, 1991, 1994), which combines a feminist with a postmodern critique of conventional conceptions of the research process, is useful. She critiques realism on the grounds that in the contemporary scene there has been a shift from an emphasis on the real – the independently existing objective world of realism, reality as self-evidently available – to an emphasis on discourses of the real – to the discursive construction of the world that takes place in the research process, how in effect research involves discourse that 'worlds' the world whilst being itself a discourse that is part of that 'worlding'; in other words, where reality is no longer self-evidently available. What this means is that we have to question the notion of 'found' worlds and accept that truth is positioned within human activities, the specific discursive practices of life. Lather argues, following Derrida (1978), that whilst the undermining of realism has inevitably meant a crisis of representation, this crisis does not so much signal the end of representation as the end of a metaphysic of pure presence. With the notion of 'text', writing is directed against the central conviction of the realist metaphysic and of Western culture – the idea of an original, organizing centre. The real cannot any longer be seen as an authorizing centre of this kind, an unmediated 'given' that grounds a representative validity – the textuality of our knowledge of the world means that it is difficult to keep on thinking in terms of unproblematically representing the world 'as it really is'.

This is a point supported in a more general way by Lemert (1997). He argues that the reality contained in empirical texts – answers to questionnaires, observed behaviours, transcripts, interviews, archives, etc. – is always textual: first, because this reality is literally inscribed in one medium or another and never recorded or used for analysis without being thus written; and second, because these texts are useful for generating knowledge only to the extent that they exist in an intertextual field with other empirical texts of the same kind, with different empirical texts, and most of all with the theoretical texts out of which sense is made of empirical texts – in other words, the research process consists not of theories pitched against reality but of texts being pitched against other texts. A point made by Leitch (1996) is also relevant here. He argues that knowledge is always 'made up' or constructed and this quality of knowledge evidences itself as inscription – it always has to be recorded or registered in some way. It follows therefore that everything we know is writing or textual; and the consequence of this is that from seeing the world 'as an orderly array of substances and things', we see it now as a constructed and contestable text. It also means that although writing (in both a wide and a narrow sense) is a necessary condition for claims to knowledge, it is also the means by which this condition can be denied. In other words, it is only through writing that the focus can be shifted from writing to that which the writing is 'about' – in other words, it is writing which makes realism possible.

This takes us back to the earlier argument, since the consequence of this is that as researchers we need to problematize representation so that we can be reflexive about the practices of representation within which we are located; in other words, we need to engage in a signifying practice that questions the grounding and effectiveness of research as a signifying practice. And now we get back again to methodology, since the problem, as we have seen, is not resolvable by deploying a better methodology, for example by being more rigorous and scientific. It is not, as Lather (1991) points out, a question of looking harder or more closely but of asking what *frames* our way of seeing when we do research – what are those spaces where visibility is constructed and from which we are *incited to see*, an incitement that marks the operation of power–knowledge formations in the research process and which makes research as a signifying practice both post-scientific or post-positivist and necessarily political.

The implication here is that there is a need to decentre validity from its traditional position as epistemological guardian – from the realist notion of the correspondence of thought with its object. Validity can then alternatively be seen as multiple, partial, endlessly deferred – what Lather (1994) calls a *transgressive* validity, which can interrupt or disrupt, even if it cannot entirely replace, a validity of correspondence. We shall explore this notion of transgressive validity further in Chapter 14. At this point, it is important to stress that it is not a matter of overthrowing and replacing conventional notions of validity, since there would then be a danger of 'transgression' itself becoming a new grounding. What transgressive validity does is to remind us that research is not simply referential. It brings to our attention how the discursive does its work through 'truth', where, because different epistemologies (or truth games) imply different relations between people, establishing truth always involves a power struggle. Furthermore, it foregrounds the limits and boundary-marking of disciplinary knowledge and questions the conventional integrity of the self as researcher – seeing this self not as a free-standing rational individual but rather as a specific subject of difference located in a representational economy.

THREE

Critical Approaches to Research

In this chapter we will look at critical approaches to research with a clear awareness that our survey will be partial and might well not do full justice to the range of approaches that could be subsumed under the term 'critical'. Indeed, that is part of the problem, for the term itself has a complex and confusing range of connotations and applications. This means that there is a great deal of disagreement as to what actually constitutes a critical approach. It tends to be the case that when critical theory is used in its capitalized form (i.e. Critical Theory), the reference is to the Frankfurt School of social theory founded in the 1930s. The concern of the social theorists associated with the School was to rethink the meaning of the Enlightenment in the light of Marxism and Freudianism at a time when the ravages of totalitarianism seemed to be making a mockery of Enlightenment ideals. As Lemert (1997: 41) puts it, 'the idea was (and is) to produce a social philosophy that could draw on these sources and remain actively critical of both them and of modern society'. The spiritual successor of the Frankfurt School is Jurgen Habermas, whose work has foregrounded the need to redefine the 'project of modernity' in the light of contemporary developments. We will discuss some of Habermas's ideas later in the chapter.

It could be argued that all critical theory contains elements of Critical Theory. This is hardly surprising, given the powerful model of the critical forged by the Frankfurt School and its successors and the continuing relevance of the attempt to both critique and redefine modernity. However, this is not to say that all critical theory is simply a gloss on Critical Theory, or that all critical approaches simply comprise modelling and enactment of the tenets of Critical Theory. The notion of the 'critical' did not originate with Critical Theory, since it can be a feature of any social theory that can be defined, to quote Lemert (1997: 68), as 'any theory of society or social life that distinguishes itself from scientific theories of society by a willingness to be critical as well as factual'. The 'critical' can therefore be said to be marked by a disengagement from the 'scientific' as conventionally conceived, with an accompanying critique of its distinguishing features such as 'objectivity', value neutrality and the strict separation between knowing subjects and objects to be known, or, to put it another way, the self and the world.

This essentially is what we foreground in our examination of critical approaches. We will take a broad view of what constitutes 'critical' and thus will include all those approaches which are critical of positivism, scientism and technical-rationality; and we will therefore include interpretive hermeneutics as well as Critical Theory in our survey, even whilst recognizing their critical differences.

INTERPRETIVIST/HERMENEUTIC APPROACHES

We noted in Chapter 2 that one of the chief characteristics of science in a positivistic mode is that it cannot be aware of its own cultural confusions. We attributed this to positivism's failure to recognize reflexivity. The consequence of this is the failure by researchers to recognize the complexity of their own practice. The reason for this is not hard to find. Positivism as an epistemology provides a powerful yet idealized model of scientific research which has shaped the pre-understandings of researchers, even those not working in the natural sciences, and hence their portrayal of what they are doing when they do research and who they are as researchers. As critics such as Kuhn and Feyerabend have pointed out, these pre-understandings and the consequent portrayals are incongruent with the practice of scientific research, which they argue can be characterized as herme-neutic and interpretive. In this chapter, taking this as our starting point, we will go on to examine the interpretive dimension in research and see how this provides the basis for a critical approach that does not so much reject science as seek to reconfigure it. Equally, what is involved is not so much a rejection of episte-mology, as a two-pronged critique – first, of positivism's idealized and universal logic of scientific explanation, and second, of its notion that one-to-one correspondence between what reality is and how it is represented can be achieved. It is argued that this is an inappropriate model for social researchers to follow, since, given the nature of the world they are researching, they must recognize not only the complexity of their practice but, more importantly, its location in culture and history.

In its hermeneutic and interpretive form, this approach has become a research tradition in its own right, powerfully shaping the doing of research in a qualitative mode. In this sense, it too has problematic elements, which we shall consider later. Historically, it has taken aim at the scientism to which positivism gives rise, the epistemological position that the natural sciences are a 'supra-historic, neutral enterprise . . . and the sole model of acquiring true knowledge' (Bleicher, 1982: 3). Gadamer (1975) disputes the powerfully held view that the natural sciences provide both the sole model of rationality and the only way of finding truth. For him, scientism makes imperialistic and unacceptable claims on behalf of the natural sciences and their methodology. He argues instead that truth is not captured by scientific method alone, and the natural sciences do not provide the one single model of rationality. In the positing of a universalistic, abstract model of rationality there is a forgetting of the conventional nature of reason, its forging in specific historical practices and cultural settings which means that it is itself in and part of an ongoing network of social beliefs, practices and discourses or 'tradition', rather than outside and separate.

One of the major criticisms that interpretivism has had to face is that any acknowledgement of the location of reason and hence of science in 'tradition' (or, to put it another way, in its own cultural confusions) immediately introduces an unacceptable subjectivity, thus destroying the 'objectivity' of science. It is certainly the case that interpretivism disagrees with the positivist emphasis upon objectivity and has sought to find a place for the 'subjective'. Yet it has also wished to remain within the broad scientific tradition and preserve the 'objectivity' of research. Much of this debate revolves around what 'objectivity' and 'subjectivity' are taken to be. The disagreement is largely about the positivist emphasis on 'objectivism' or the realist metaphysic of a world existing independently of knowers, the separating of knowing subjects from objects. On the other hand, for interpretivism it is not a matter of the world being whatever we want it to be – a position that could be crudely called 'subjectivism'. It has sought rather to provide alternative yet epistemologically legitimate approaches to research – in other words, approaches that are still scientific but not positivistic and not captured by the realist metaphysic. Gadamer argues that, for example, knowledge cannot be objective in a positivist sense but must necessarily include a 'subjective' element. Understanding something is always 'prejudiced' in the sense that it is a process of requiring an initial projection that anticipates meaning and which orients the process. This initial projection or pre-understanding is part of the subject's situatedness – the subject's location and standpoint in history, society and culture. Thus, as social beings, we cannot help but be subjective, yet this is itself located in the 'objective' rather than in psychological dispositions.

In interpretivism, research takes everyday experience and ordinary life as its subject-matter and asks how meaning is constructed and social interaction negotiated in social practices. Human action is inseparable from meaning, and experiences are classified and ordered through interpretive frames, through pre-understandings mediated by 'tradition'. The task of research then becomes to work with, and make sense of, the world, through the frames and pre-understandings of the researched rather than the categories of the social sciences.

The process of meaning-making and negotiation over meaning is always a practical matter for individuals in the sense that it is located in their social practices. Situations are interpreted and, whilst these interpretations looked at 'objectively' may be faulty or misleading, they reveal for researchers the shared and constructed nature of social reality – and this would have been missed had the researchers been 'objective' in a positivist sense. Positivism can therefore be critiqued on the grounds that it fails to understand the multiplicity and complexity of the 'lifeworld' of individuals. This 'lifeworld' is instead reduced to an oppressive uniformity through the imposition of scientific categories. Given, then, that the field of study is the meaningful actions of individuals and the social construction of reality, the social sciences must be distinct from the natural sciences, with different methods, different ways of explaining and different criteria about what constitutes valid knowledge. Thus explaining the social world involves understanding or making sense of it, and hence involves understanding the meanings that both construct and are constructed by interactive human behaviour. The goal of research becomes that of providing interpretations of human actions and social practices within the context of meaningful, culturally specific arrangements.

If all sense-seeking and sense-making is through culturally and historically located interpretive frames, then the knowledge of subjects is perspective-bound and partial, i.e. relative to these frameworks. Gadamer (1975) argues that it is impossible to separate oneself as a researcher from the historical and cultural context that defines one's interpretive frame since both the 'subject' and the 'object' of research are located in pre-understood worlds. In contrast to the realist metaphysic, there is no object-in-itself independent of a context of knowing and of the knowing activities of subjects. Frames (or pre-understandings) constitute 'the initial directedness of our whole ability to experience . . . the conditions whereby we experience something – whereby what we encounter says something to us' (ibid: 173).

Underlying Gadamer's argument is the notion of a universal hermeneutics – where understanding precedes methodical knowing, where understanding always involves interpretation and where interpretation is therefore universal. Interpretation is not, however, arbitrary – one possible sense of 'subjective' – but, as we have just noted, takes place through interpretive frames which are themselves located within the background of all our beliefs and practices. One implication of this is that frames can never be fully and definitively specified, since any such specification would itself be an interpretation that must presuppose a background of assumptions, presuppositions, beliefs and practices. There is therefore no origin, no ultimate presence which can be an authorizing centre. Such an origin can never be fully specified and the background or Gadamer's 'tradition' can never be something of which both researchers and researched can ever be fully aware. Even apparently simple actions, such as arm-raising, can only be understood in terms of an immersion and inseparability from a background and are therefore never fully specifiable.

What is also implied is that no interpretation can ever be uniquely correct, because this would presuppose that there is an interpretation which is 'authentic' and originary. But there is no logocentric presence, no bedrock 'fact of the matter' or empirical 'given' which could be appealed to as the court of last resort in deciding between different interpretations. This means that understanding is always circular because it is always already an interpretation. The consequence is that there can be no standardized method or algorithm or theory of meaning which can function as criteria that produce a uniquely correct interpretation, or definitively settle the validity of any one interpretation in conflict with others – and this is the reason why interpretations can never be 'objective' in a positivist sense.

Furthermore, as Bohman (1991) points out, since social action is the outcome of knowledgeable and reflexive actors interacting with other knowledgeable and reflexive actors, explanations of social action must always remain indeterminate – in other words, no explanation is ever definitive, but always contains a capacity for resisting closure. In contrast, a positivist methodology always requires a closure. As we have seen, any understanding of human actions that purported to be a final and closed explanation would be necessarily incomplete. For example, if we were seeking to understand an action such as arm-raising purely in terms of physical movements or even of the stated intentions of the actor, we would be missing out, in the name of closure, so much that was relevant to this action that our explanation would be impoverished and incomplete.

Thus indeterminacy is present because of the 'partiality' of any particular interpretation, its meaning being dependent on something beyond itself in the 'background'. At the same time, this background should not be seen as a reified object, since it can only be manifested through partial interpretations. For example, the meaning of a book is manifested through each of its chapters (the parts), yet each chapter's meaning depends on the meaning of the whole book. At the same time, there is also a background which comes into play – of practices of reading, of culture and history, for example about what constitutes a 'book'. This background is meaningfully 'present', but also absent from the awareness of the reader. This determination of meaning in the interaction of part and whole against an unconscious background is the hermeneutic circle. But it is important to note, as Bohman does, that the circular and perspectival qualities of interpretation which make it always partial and incomplete are not something extraneous, but that which makes interpretation possible – in other words, its condition of possibility. From this comes a conception of knowledge-formation as iterative and spiral rather than as linear and cumulative as portrayed in positivist epistemology.

As a social practice, research is itself a meaningful human action constructed through interpretive frames. Researchers are also in the sense-making business, so unlike the situation in the natural sciences, in social research both researchers and research subjects are sense-makers and knowers. Research therefore involves interpreting the actions of those who are themselves interpreters. It is an interpretation of interpretations. Several questions now arise for the researcher. Researchers are themselves immersed in a background or 'tradition' that gives meaning to their actions as researchers, yet of which they are largely unaware – and according to Kuhn (1970) this is the case even with researchers in the natural sciences (in a sense, Kuhnian paradigms can be seen as 'traditions'). But of course, as we have seen, 'tradition' cannot here be construed purely in a narrow sense of a research tradition. In the light of this, therefore, the notion of the individual researcher standing outside the world in order to properly understand it seems highly questionable. Caught within the hermeneutic circle, researchers must find it impossible to adopt such a stance.

Any methodical enquiry has as its starting point the pre-understandings that subjects have of that which they are researching simply through the fact of it sharing a world with them. Thus the purpose which motivates and animates enquiry, the carving out of a field of study and the emergence of criteria and standards by which scientific study is evaluated are all dependent on the historical situatedness of scientific activity and therefore on the pre-understandings of researchers. But this immediately brings us back to the problem of objectivity touched on earlier. How can researchers, as interpreters or meaning producers, be 'objective' about the meanings produced by those they are researching? Furthermore, how can they themselves be 'objective' in the sense of not falling into arbitrary subjectivism? One answer to this problem has been that, although researchers must recognize their situatedness, they must also 'bracket', i.e. temporarily suspend, their subjectivity and explanatory frames.

Yet this position is not altogether satisfactory, and an alternative suggested by Gadamer shows why. He argues that it is impossible to escape from our 'pre-understandings' even temporarily. But at the same time, it is precisely through the interplay between one's interpretive frames or pre-understandings and the elements of the actions one is trying to understand that knowledge is developed. In other words, one's pre-understandings, far from being closed prejudices or biases (as they are thought of in positivist epistemology), actually make one more open-minded because in the process of interpretation and understanding they are put at risk, tested and modified through the encounter with what one is trying to understand. So rather than bracketing or 'suspending' them, we should use them as the essential starting point for acquiring knowledge. To know, one must be aware of one's pre-understandings even though one cannot transcend them. At the same time, however, whilst they are an essential starting point, they need to be left open to modification in the course of the research.

Since knowledge always involves interpretation within historical and cultural contexts, truths are historical rather than abstract, contingent rather than determinate. Furthermore, they are grasped not by eliminating subjectivity but through the intersubjective relationship between the knowing subject and the object to be known. Knowledge is not a matter of subject and object becoming identical but of them entering into a necessary dialectical relationship. The questions that researchers ask arise from their experiences and concerns located in sociocultural traditions. As Westkott (1990) points out, the answers emerge not only from the way that objects confirm and/or expand these experiences but also from the ways that they oppose or remain silent about them. What is involved, then, is a dialogue or what Gadamer calls a 'fusion of horizons', where knowledge is an unpredictable emergent rather than a controlled outcome.

Here an analogy between literary texts and social phenomena becomes productive, since both are complex systems of meaningful elements that are in need of interpretation. As Hollinger (1994) argues, behind interpretivism is the view that human life is essentially historical and that human societies and behaviour need to be read like a complex text. Thus what is involved in understanding is translation, empathy, dialogue, participant observation and 'thick' description. As a hermeneutic enquiry the task for research becomes one of working out as many meanings as possible of a complex social life. So if social phenomena can be read as and like texts, Gadamer argues that understanding a text is only partly a function of the historical situation of the interpreter, as there is also the 'subject-matter' itself which must be given due weight.

In the fusion of horizons, the term 'horizon' refers to one's standpoint or situatedness (in time, place, culture, gender, ethnicity, etc.) and the standpoint or situatedness of that which one is trying to understand. The fusion results from an understanding which is grounded in both standpoints, neither of which can be bracketed out. One could say that a fusion of horizons occurs when 'authors' and 'readers', both of whom are historically situated, create shared meanings. Because it is situated, every horizon is inevitably limited, but it is also open to connecting with other horizons (perspectives, standpoints). The resulting fusion is an enlargement or broadening of one's own horizon which leaves open the possibility for continual reinterpretation and different meanings as horizons move and change. The fusion of horizons constitutes a standard of objectivity which can function as an alternative to the objectivity of positivist–empiricist epistemology. It is the outcome of intersubjective agreement where different and conflicting interpretations are played out and possibly harmonized. Through the comparing and contrasting of various interpretations, a consensus can be achieved despite differences, indeed *because* of differences.

This implies that there is nothing which potentially cannot be understood. But it also implies that understanding is not simply a knowledge of objects but also an awareness that everything cannot be methodically known – there are things which just simply fall outside the understanding of positivistic science. Interpretive or hermeneutic understanding is a learning process involving dialogue between researchers and researched – a dialogue which is always ongoing and incomplete.

We started off this chapter by referring to the arguments of those such as Kuhn that the natural sciences incorporate a hermeneutic or interpretive dimension in their practice, and in that sense are not too dissimilar to the social sciences. Rorty (1980) argues that scientific knowledge is not a reflection or 'mirror' of the world and science cannot seek to claim legitimacy on the grounds that it is the only way of knowing what the world is 'really' like. As Lyotard (1984) has shown, science gets its legitimacy from quite another source, from the grand narratives of modernity which are themselves not open to scientific proof. Science itself does not exist outside history and culture. The sciences may be an effective vocabulary in the game of prediction and control, but they are not a privileged or final vocabulary, even less a model for other forms of knowledge and action.

The fact that both researchers and researched engage in interpretive practices means that the social sciences and social research cannot help but be engaged in a dialogue with its subject matter. In other words, it cannot help but be reflexive, although this is not to say that it always is. That it is not is largely due to the influence of positivism and technical-rationality. Theoretical knowledge is floated off into a contextual-free vacuum, the 'stuff' of research is detached from its locating background and researchers are cast as ideal knowing machines who can know the world only by being outside it, even though they still seek to 'master' it.

Interpretivism is a popular approach to research for educators, because in emphasizing the social actor and her/his situatedness it seems to offer a more fruitful and 'human' way of doing research. This is reinforced by the focus on everyday practices which offers a great deal of scope for classroom research and ethnographic field research generally. Through the foregrounding of interaction, meaning and social construction it appears to avoid both the scientism and objectivism of positivist approaches and the remote theoreticism of critical theory's more structural emphasis. However, as we have noted in Chapter 2, there are problems with interpretivism. For many educators, particularly those with a strong commitment to notions of the sovereign self and its innate capacity for self-direction, notions such as the hermeneutic circle and unconscious background would not be readily acceptable. Certainly, for those concerned with policy-making and looking for 'steers' from research, notions of indeterminacy and necessary incompleteness are highly problematic. For radical educators, interpretivist emphasis on understanding the world is secured at the expense of changing it. They would argue that interpretive approaches merely perpetuate positivism's hierarchy of knowers and doers, theory and practice, and in so doing serve to maintain the world as it is.

CRITICAL THEORY

As we noted earlier, one sense in which critical theory is 'critical' is that it challenges the positivist approach to research. But it is also critical of the interpretive approach, seeing it, as much as positivism, as being enmeshed in dominant ideology. The aim of Critical Theory is emancipation, so it is critical in the sense that it does not simply seek to generate knowledge of the world as it is but to detect and unmask beliefs and practices that limit human freedom, justice and democracy and to engage in action that brings these about. The task of educational research and practice is thus seen as transformative in relation to both individuals and the social world – research is seen as needing to be part of the process of establishing the conditions for the rational conduct of social life.

Habermas's (1987) argument concerning the links between knowledge and social interests or basic social needs can also be applied to different research traditions, given their role as knowledge producers. The natural sciences and positivist tendencies in the social sciences employ technical-rationality. Given its instrumental means/ends character, Habermas describes this kind of knowledge as guided by a technical problem-solving interest where the concern is with generalization and prediction and the need for control. On the other hand, the interpretive or hermeneutic sciences, including some of the social sciences, employ practical modes of reasoning where methodology does not consist of following invariant procedures and rules of method. As we have seen, these sciences recognize the significance of context and meaning and their concern is with understanding and illumination and the need for communication.

Yet despite their differences, neither has an interest in changing the world, neither has an emancipatory goal. Habermas therefore identifies a third type of knowledge interest that is associated with Critical Theory. This interest is emancipatory and involves the unmasking of ideologies that maintain the *status quo* by restricting access to the means of gaining knowledge and hence to the means of raising consciousness or awareness about the oppressive material conditions and structures that lead to the failure to fulfil basic social needs. Empowerment involves understanding the causes of powerlessness, recognizing systemic oppressive forces and acting collectively to change the conditions of life. Critical theory in this sense therefore involves both ideology critique and what Habermas calls the 'organization of enlightenment', or the taking of rational action on the basis of knowledge. Both ideology critique and the organization of enlightenment are forms of social learning. The former is learning which functions to transform identities so that individuals see themselves differently, and the latter is learning relating to what needs to be done to change social contexts. One implication of all this, therefore, is that there can be no 'objective' knowledge in the sense of knowledge gained from a neutral or perspective-free position. Knowledge is always socially constructed and geared to a particular interest, a technical problem-solving interest, a practical communicative interest or a critical emancipatory interest – and where an interest is manifested through actions informed by different types of rationality.

The critical emancipatory interest seeks to remove structurally rooted obstacles because it is these which give rise to what Habermas calls 'systematically distorted communication'. For Habermas, communication is a basic social need. He argues that all human communication implicitly involves the making of validity claims. A communicative transaction involves four such claims – that what is said and done is intelligible, truthful, justified and sincere. Given this, Habermas argues that undistorted communication involves a situation where all four validity claims can be justified or redeemed – a situation which he refers to as the 'ideal speech situation'. The implication, then, is that communicative transactions should be such as to allow the parties involved to make successful validity claims. It follows, therefore, that the task is to create the right conditions for this to happen – in other words, to create an ideal speech situation.

Habermas sees the ideal speech situation as involving rational agreement reached through critical discussion, an agreement or consensus which can be distinguished from one arising from custom, faith or coercion – a critical dialogue conducted through known public criteria. Here justifications become explicit as people talk about their reasons for what they do but not in terms simply of their desires – for example, 'I did X because I wanted to'- or because of the demands of their context – for example, 'I did X because I had to.' In the ideal speech situation all participants have an understanding of the technical issues involved coupled with a procedural understanding of how to act appropriately and a competence to participate fully and equally. The ideal speech situation, with its absence of external and internal constraints, is characterized by openness and a commitment to deep explanation, where each participant has an equal chance of participating and therefore where all validity claims can be successfully redeemed. In this way, any consensus achieved through dialogue will be based on the force of the better argument rather than the force of ideology. In the ideal speech situation knowledge, truth and emancipation become inseparable. There is a uniting of micro- and macro-levels, for it is clear that the conditions and outcomes of successful intersubjective dialogue are also the conditions for a successful democratic society.

However, all this poses a difficult problem, for the question arises of how it is possible to tell whether critical rationality is not itself ideological. Habermas argues that emancipation depends on conducting life rationally, but how is this rationality itself to be justified? What is it that makes critical rationality rational? The problem is compounded by critical theory's challenge to positivist notions of objectivity. Both interpretivists and critical theorists argue that objectivity is not primarily a matter of having the right methods. Both foreground the importance of critical dialogue, one interpretivist version of which is found in the notion of 'fusion of horizons'. For critical theorists, however, this is not enough, for they want to argue that this dialogue has to be free from and unconstrained by ideology. But where is the ideology-free position to be found to mount a rational critique of ideology?

It is the ideal speech situation that again comes into play as a counter to these difficulties. Habermas argues that the ideal speech situation is presupposed in any discursive context and is an essential element of the critical dialogue which redeems validity claims. Communication necessarily presupposes the four validity claims of intelligibility, truth, sincerity and appropriateness by the very act of its taking place. Indeed, the very notion of a language makes no sense without some notion of an ideal speech situation. To engage in dialogue whilst repudiating it is to fall into contradiction. It follows, therefore, that the values and criteria of the ideal speech situation are universal – they are present in any language and any dialogue, and are in effect context-free. The ideal speech situation defines a society where all basic social needs have been fulfilled. In this sense, it is counter-factual, but this is not the end of the matter, for the ideal speech situation, can function as a norm or regulative ideal, an idealization of rational practice, even though most actual conditions of social interaction and communication are nothing like this. In this sense, it provides a critical measure of the inadequacies of existing forms of interaction and practices. Thus actual situations can be examined (an important task of research) to ascertain the degree to which they deviate from an ideal speech situation and appropriate action can be taken to bring them closer to the ideal. But more significantly than this, the ideal speech situation seems to provide the ideology-free position from which ideology can itself be rationally critiqued. It is universal and transcendent, it provides public and shareable criteria for justifying and choosing, it is 'objective' but not in the sense of either positivist or interpretivist objectivity, and it cannot be denied without falling into substantive contradiction. As such, it provides the rational justification for critical rationality, removing from the latter any accusation that it may itself be just another ideology.

However, the fact that the ideal speech situation is rarely if ever present poses other difficulties. Should researchers endeavour to bring it about? If research is not to be either an instrument for the further dominance of technical-rationality or for the furtherance of human understanding and communication, then something else is needed. For critical theorists this something else is praxis or informed, committed action oriented to change and transformation. Dialogue is a necessary but not a sufficient condition for emancipation, since praxis is also required for realizing the latter. This means that research in the critical theory mode is not simply about 'finding out' or increasing understanding but about helping to create the right conditions for critical dialogue and emancipatory action. Research and praxis become inseparable or, to put it another way, research becomes praxis. Here, then, researchers cannot simply stand aside and adopt a passive disinterested stance – on the contrary, they have to be very much in, and part of, the world they are researching. Researchers are not scientists working in a laboratory or even scientists in the field seeking to understand social life. Whilst they approach their work with scientific rigour and whilst they seek to understand, they also seek to transform.

> [research is] structured in relation to our efforts to construct a mode of learning and a conception of knowledge that may enhance the possibility of collectively constituted thought and action which seeks to transform the relations of power that construct people's lives. (Simon and Dippo, 1986: 196)

Critical theory and the approach it offers has resonated with both educational practitioners and researchers. Its discourse of basic social needs, of distortions and of false consciousness, and its foregrounding of critical dialogue and praxis, provide an appealing basis for theory and practice, particularly for educators committed to social action and change. Its refusal to separate research and knowledge (theory) from action (practice) demolishes the debilitating tension between theory and practice. An approach informed by critical theory provides one possible answer to both the epistemological question of what constitutes valid knowledge, and the ethical question of how it can best be used. Its aim of an empowerment in the cause of emancipation provides a purposive goal and a moral dimension for educational research and practice. Above all, critical theory provides a standard by which the present can be evaluated and, in the sense that the empirically existing world is never going to match up to that standard, it provides an endless resource for research and action.

However, critical theory is not unproblematic. Although it seeks to unmask distortions and constraints, it itself offers a very partial and distorted view of human experience and social interaction. It uses a very modernist and rationalistic discourse which privileges the place of rationality, and although this is not positivism's narrow version, it is none the less a totalizing and excluding rationality which in its own way is equally oppressive. What is presented is clearly a very different conception of the nature of research from mainstream modernist conceptions, particularly of the positivist–empiricist variety, yet the emphasis on reason means that critical theory is more in the business of redefining than in that of challenging modernist categories and hierarchies – and this is probably due to its Critical Theory heritage.

Earlier we pointed out how the ideal speech situation was the condition of possibility of language as a communicative tool. We saw how as a consequence it provides the justification for critical rationality, or the answer to why critical rationality is not itself yet another oppressive ideology. But this now suggests a further question which is to do with what makes the ideal speech situation possible. As Parker (1997) points out, the most plausible answer is undistorted language, because if language is distorted then the rationality that constitutes the ideal speech situation becomes distorted and in effect then does become yet another ideology.

What is required for language to be undistorted? Such a language would have to be pure and transparent – a language free of the distorting effects of particular practices, readings and interpretations. In other words, what is being asked for here is a totally decontextualized language which can fulfil its referential function without vagueness, variation or ambiguity. It is not difficult to realize that such a view of language is highly problematic. Apart from the impossibility of finding such a language, it cannot even be posited as a norm or regulative ideal, since even if it were achievable it would actually end all communication rather than undistort it. It is precisely because language is distorted that we can communicate through it, so any realization of the ideal speech situation, far from making for undistorted communication, would actually stop all communication in its tracks. Thus the clarity and transparency which Critical Theory seeks and which it believes it can achieve in the furtherance of emancipation is itself a form of distortion, a process that would end up destroying that which it seeks to enhance. Curiously enough, whilst Critical Theory distances itself from positivism, its stance on the possibility and desirability of a pure, transparent and unambiguous language is something shared in common.

Related to this are problems arising from the commitment to an emancipatory project construed in a naturalistic and universalizing way – that is in terms of concepts of basic needs and emancipatory goals. The assumption is that as universals they are invariant in their meaning and interpretation across cultural contexts, readily discernible by a rational mind purged of ideology. Such a position must in the end be sustainable only by assuming the possibility of a pure and undistorted language. Yet as Parker strongly argues, critical theory is itself constructed through metaphors such as purification, clarification, depth, essences, distorting surfaces – and the metaphoric is virtually the paradigm case of 'impure' language. Thus it would be possible to argue that critical theory deconstructs itself by understanding itself as literal, as being about the need for and effects of a pure undistorted language, yet only being able to speak of this metaphorically.

Of course, it is easy enough to argue against Habermas that Critical Theory and the emphasis on the ideal speech situation is unrealistic. This is particularly so in relation to its failure to recognize differences in argumentative ability and expertise, and hence differences in the power to participate in dialogue that are not simply due to external constraints. At the same time, the assumption that modernity has an essence which is still unrealized but could be realized if only we were more rational sounds more like wishful thinking than a rational argument. In a sense, we are now too much influenced by the postmodern and post-structural critique of scholars such as Foucault, Derrida and Lyotard of invariant essences, originating presences, and universalizing emancipatory discourses; hence the tendency is to regard the project of critical theory as naive and problematic.

Furthermore, we now recognize that such projects and their associated discourses do not always have the effect intended – in fact, very often quite the opposite. Gore (1993: 61) deploys Foucault's notion of regimes of truth to argue that 'critical theory has its own power–knowledge nexus which in particular contexts and particular historical moments will operate in ways that are oppressive and repressive to people within and/or outside'. Critical theorists believe that their role is to encourage and seek rational critique, and to enforce the norms governing rational discourse – and all this in the cause of emancipation. It is not too difficult to see how this position could easily slip into one of mastery and how critical theory can itself so easily become a 'masterful' discourse. This possibility is heightened by the failure to foreground reflexivity. Here, the problem is not so much that critical researchers do not recognize the need to ensure that the right conditions for dialogue are present in their own practice; a significant place is allocated to reflection, but critical theorists are not required to be reflexive, they are not required to submit their own position to critical scrutiny and examine the nature and effects of the power relations, operating 'behind their backs' but still none the less present in their emancipatory projects.

ACTION RESEARCH

Whilst at one level it may seem odd to include action research in our survey of critical approaches to research, there are none the less good reasons for doing so. First, whilst it is an approach to research in its own right, it is also a concrete way of doing research that has proved to be very influential in the world of education. In this context, it has been 'critical' because given its focus on improving practice, it has found itself directly challenging a whole number of traditions. The list is long, but it includes deeply embedded institutional and curricular practices, the theory–practice distinction, the academic model of research and the notion of researchers as methodological and substantive experts. As Stronach and MacLure (1997: 128–9) argue, action research has drawn both its power and its problems of legitimation from 'its challenge to the customary dispositions of "privilege" in the unequal relations of dualism – between theory and practice, subjectivity and objectivity, academic and practitioner'.

A second and related reason, one that is central to the argument of this chapter, is that action research constitutes a powerful critique of positivism, technical-rationality and their associated academic and institutional discourses. What is interesting about this is that this critique has been most effective through being exemplified in the practice of action research rather than in its theorization. This is not to say that there is no theory of and in action research or that the practice of action research does not raise crucial epistemological issues. It is, however, to emphasize that action research critically depends on its doing for its being, and it is through the critique immanent in the doing that action research has been able to challenge and mitigate the oppressive features of positivistic and technical-rational research and theory for teachers and others who have been its main beneficiaries. This is also understandable in the light of the historical development of action research. Its origins, in the educational world at least, lie in a curriculum reform that sought to make academic research relevant to practitioners' problems. With this came the recognition that teachers could themselves be researchers doing research, geared to their practice, and of a kind radically different from the dominant 'scientific' research of the time.

There is therefore a clear 'critical' dimension in action research, although, as we shall go on to see, this is not a necessary feature and is certainly not fully realized in all cases. At this point, however, it is appropriate to consider how action research has been conceptualized. Here, for example, is a definition provided by Ebbutt (1985: 156) – 'the systematic study of attempts to change and improve educational practice by groups of participants by means of their own practical actions and by means of their own reflections upon the effects of their own actions'. Here is another from Elverno *et al.* (1997) – 'action research is explicitly a democratic form of research aimed at social change that respects both the problems and goals of those within organisations/institutions undergoing change'. Although both echo a similar spirit of action research, there are none the less significant differences. Both emphasize the practitioner base of action research and the orientation towards change. It is interesting, however, that Elverno *et al.* refer to 'social change', whilst Ebbutt speaks only of changing and improving 'educational practice'. There is also a common emphasis on researchers and practitioners working collaboratively together, and the significance of this is that neither even uses the term 'researcher'.

In their definition, Elverno *et al.* explicitly talk of action research as respecting the 'intelligence and goals' of practitioners. Elaborating on their definition, they refer to an important feature of action research as mobilizing research expertise in a non-authoritarian way. They foreground the importance of the 'team' who jointly agree upon all phases of the research process. They see as one of the fundamental assumptions of action research that no one has an inherent right to do research. What they mean by this is that academic researchers do not have an unconditional right to research whatever they want as they want simply because they are academic researchers. Rather, research must be conducted in the interests of, and in collaboration with, those affected by it. One could argue that Elverno *et al.* are defining the ethics of action research rather than its epistemology, although this is not to say that such an ethic does not have epistemological consequences. Perhaps more specifically, it is to say that action research does not allow a separation of the ethical and the epistemological nor a privileging of the latter over the former as is the case in positivistic approaches to research.

This is not to say that the epistemological issue is unimportant. There is always a perennial question about action research – is it really research? Cohen and Manion (1989), whilst stressing its situational and participatory features, argue that because it focuses on a specific problem in a specific setting it is not rigorously scientific, although they add that it is preferable to subjective problem-solving. They also claim that because data are situationally specific they cannot be extended beyond the specific case. Hence action research suffers from problems of validity, lacking as it is in generalizability. Winter (1989), however, argues that action research should not be judged in a positivistic way, but that a validity model is needed, different from that offered by positivism, since without such a model action research will always be seen as an incompetent and suspect version of 'real' science. He therefore puts forward six principles – reflexive critique, dialectical critique, collaborative resource, risk, plural structure, theory–practice transformation – which can function as alternative criteria for validating action research.

The assumption in action research is that human beings are knowledgeable about their own situation, and the fact that they are in their situation, and not detached from it as the scientific researcher is supposed to be, does not thereby disqualify their knowledge. The problem is really one of 'knowledge that's not acknowledged', as one of the participants in a 'Teachers as Researchers' project notes (Stronach and MacLure, 1997: 118). Equally, the fact that their knowledge is quotidian, practical and often tacit does not thereby render that knowledge invalid. As Elverno *et al.* point out, practitioners are capable of analysing their own actions, and no outside researcher can ever be as knowledgeable about a practice as a team of insiders. These assumptions mark the intertwining of the ethical and epistemological positions that is such a significant feature of action research.

One cannot help but feel that Ebbutt's definition is more 'technical' in the sense that the highlighting of a critical dimension is missing. Whilst one would not wish to imply that this is intentional, it is perhaps not coincidental. As we noted earlier, the critical dimension is not a necessary feature of action research. As has been noted in the literature, there are many varieties of action research. Elverno *et al.* for example, note three possible variants: for altering structures of power, for enhancing participation in and co-generation of organizational decisions, and for furthering individual awareness and self-realization through working in groups. Coming at the matter slightly differently, Carr and Kemmis (1986) also list three possible variants: technical action research, which is concerned with improving the efficiency and effectiveness of systems, organizations and institutions where there is an 'external' agenda and no sense of collective responsibility; practical action research, which is concerned with the improvement and change of practitioner understandings and actions, but where again there is no sense of collective responsibility; and emancipatory action research, concerned with improving and changing practitioner understandings, but where this time there is collaborative work in and collective responsibility for removing internal and external constraints.

What emerges from this is that whilst it may be possible to map the common features and characteristics of action research, action research is not one single 'thing'. There is a wide variation in the goals and practice of action research, and whilst it could be argued that all action research is oriented towards the change and improvement of practice, not all has a critical dimension. One could envisage this in terms of a spectrum, with Carr and Kemmis's technical action research at one end and their emancipatory action research at the other. Technical action research could be seen as having elements of technical-rationality, and this is clearly an influential way of doing action research. This is perhaps also why Cohen and Manion refer to action research as being implemented within the existing constraints of the organization – what Bryant (1996) refers to as 'accommodative' action research. Equally, practical action research and the enhancing of participation in organizational decision-making advocated by Elverno *et al.* could be seen as being halfway along the spectrum, where the emphasis is on change and improvement but without a necessary emancipatory goal. It is also the kind of action research which Elliott (1991) has in mind when he refers to it as improving practice through the realization of processual values. Directly attacking technical-rationality, he argues that practice is not simply a technical matter of how to achieve a given end most effectively but is inevitably value-laden. It is concerned not simply with the pragmatic, with what is possible, but also with what is desirable, and thus both ends and the means to achieve ends are co-implicated within value-frameworks.

The most obvious critical dimension is that spelt out by Carr and Kemmis in their notion of emancipatory action research, which, it would probably be safe to say, they regard as the only authentic form of action research. One can argue for this, because they seem to see action research very much in Habermasian terms – indeed, the very designation 'emancipatory' would strongly suggest this. For them, action research carried out by practitioners into their own practices is a participatory and democratic form of educational research for educational improvement – a form of practical enquiry but with emancipatory potential. It involves three inter-related and interactive aspects – the improvement of practice, the improvement of the practitioner's understanding of practice, and the improvement of the situation in which practice takes place or, to summarize more succinctly, actions, understandings and settings. The process of collabora-tive work is a spiral of planning, acting, observing and reflecting centred on the interplay of action and critique.

For Carr and Kemmis, action research is about practice as praxis, in the sense of both its study and its exemplification, where participants/researchers come to understand themselves better, become better informed about their situation, and act collectively and responsibly to bring about a particular kind of change. Whereas Elliott (1991) stresses that the fundamental aim of action research is to improve practice rather than to produce knowledge, Carr and Kemmis see action research as being about both, a position endorsed by Winter (1989) when he refers to the basic unity of theoretical and practical knowledge in action research, with both working together to attain the goal of emancipation. Whereas Elliott stresses the realization of processual values and Cohen and Manion talk of change that accommodates to the constraints of an organization, Carr and Kemmis talk of substantive change which removes constraints.

It seems clear that Carr and Kemmis construct their understanding of action research very much through Habermas' model of an ideal speech situation. In a sense, what is involved in the process of action research is the redemption of validity claims, a process characterized by the praxis (informed committed action) of all participants. For them, action research therefore can be the nearest thing to realizing the ideal speech situation, although they are also well aware that the empirical practice of action research falls far short of this. But again what Carr and Kemmis try to do, and again they are following Habermas in doing this, is to construct a norm or regulative ideal for action research which both prescribes how action research should be and the criteria for critiquing its actual conduct and goals.

We have already noted the problematic aspects of the ideal speech situation. At that time, we located the problem in the assumption of a pure transparent language as its condition of possibility, and yet it is in the making of this assumption that the whole Habermasian theorization of the ideal speech situation deconstructs itself. The problem with Carr and Kemmis's theorization is slightly different, although with many similar elements. Here perhaps we can draw on Stronach and MacLure (1997) for elaboration. They point out that action research draws its power from the hierarchical binary oppositions mentioned earlier, and yet at the same time it seeks to transcend these oppositions by reversing the hierarchies, so that, for example, practice is privileged over theory, the practitioner over the researcher. Whilst this is a first deconstructive step in dissolving the oppressive power of these binary oppositions, action research does not take the next step, which is to understand them as always present, and indeed necessarily always present, in a conflicting yet interactive way. Each pole of the opposition needs the other, but must always remain 'other'. To merely reverse the hierarchy does not remove binary oppositions but creates the possibility for the formation of another one to take the place of the one dissolved – and, moreover, one which is ultimately unsustainable.

Thus action research attempts to counter the oppressive hierarchical power of binary oppositions by reconciling the opposites. But in doing this it locates itself in an economy of the same which rejects the otherness or radical alterity which cannot be reconciled. This means that in critical action research emancipation has to be constructed in terms of an economy of sameness, where emancipation becomes the same for all regardless of difference and can only be brought about by processes of rational consensus which converge to the same. Consequently, emancipation has to be understood in ways which are oppressive. This is why the problems endemic to Carr and Kemmis's theorization of action research, although different in some respects to Habermas's need for a pure transparent language as the basis of the ideal speech situation, are very similar in the significant respect of rejecting difference.

From their 'Teachers as Researchers' project, which included interview studies of the life histories of action researchers who had once been located in the school but were now in the academy, Stronach and MacLure (1997: 116) argue that these researchers embodied in themselves the oppositional dilemmas inherent in action research. Their life narratives were constructed around these dilemmas and they, like action research itself, constantly rehearsed them. Yet they also constantly sought a reconciliation of these structuring dilemmas, which in their narratives revolved around 'the notion of the self and its romantic/rational adventure leading to triumph over the adversity of contradictions'. This too is reflected in the project of action research within which they were located, where reconciliations are sought 'in which the interests of those who previously lived antagonistically on opposite sides of the boundary will find a new space in which their differences can be resolved or dissolved' (ibid.).

Underpinning action research, therefore, is a particular notion of the singular and centred self which, despite experiencing dilemmas, tensions and constraints, can none the less reconcile and transcend these. Such a self is in one sense emancipated and in other sense not, caught as it is in an economy of the same. The story of reconciliation told by action research and embodied in the lives of action researchers is one of fixing a singular and stable identity in the face of the fragmentation and difference that doing action research involves. This prompts the question – does action research work by 'consuming the ungovernable alterity of the "client" [i.e. teachers as participants] leaving in its place this dead smelly thing called teacher identity'? (ibid: 130). Does action research consume its otherness in order to produce the singular centred self?

One of the most significant characteristics of action research is its flexibility, which does allow for alternative ways of doing research and alternative ways of writing. Whilst most action research in practice has utilized the case study as its preferred method, there is no inherent reason why this should be the only method. This flexibility is no coincidence, particularly if one sees action research in a more postmodern way as a hybrid, as a 'boundary-dweller' and border crosser. To see action research in this way does, in our view, do greater justice to its rich diversity. It allows working with postmodern notions of multiple selves and economies of difference whilst still allowing participants to free themselves from the oppressive certainties of positivist theory and the tyranny of technical-rationality.

FOUR

Ways of Thinking

In order to fully understand the nature of educational research, we need to surface, as we have been doing in the last two chapters, those epistemological and ontological frameworks which underpin processes, strategies and methods. In addition, we need to make explicit the way in which educational researchers move, sometimes in a seemingly effortless manner, from preconception, through data description to postconception or summary of findings. Four approaches have been developed: induction, deduction, retroduction and abduction.

INDUCTION

A much used approach in educational research is that of grounded theory developed by Glaser and Strauss (1967) in their seminal work, *The Discovery of Grounded Theory*, and as we will see, modified by them and later collaborators in response to persistent criticisms. Bartlett and Payne (1997) plot the way in which grounded theory developed from its early emphasis on induction through to an acceptance that researchers bring with them to the setting a variety of epistemological and ontological assumptions which they test against the empirical world. However, it should not be assumed that grounded theorists have abandoned altogether their inductive orientation, and this approach is essentially one of discovery – theory develops from the data which are collected and not by the testing of deductively formulated hypotheses.

Grounded theorists argue that their method is both an analytical one and a specific way of understanding the social world. They, for example,

> share a conviction with many other qualitative researchers that the usual canons of 'good science' (... significance, theory-observation compatibility, generalisability, consistency, reproducibility, precision and verification ...) should be retained, but require redefinition in order to fit the realities of qualitative research and the complexities of social phenomena. (Strauss and Corbin, 1990: 4)

It is an interesting question as to whether they have moved fundamentally from a position which could be shared with positivist researchers.

Bartlett and Payne (1997) summarize grounded theory procedures as shown in Table 4.1.

Table 4.1: Grounded theory procedures

Process	Activity	Comments
i.	Collect data	Any source of textual data may be used but semi-structured interviews or observations are the most common
ii.	Transcribe data	It is necessary to produce full transcriptions of the data in order to analyse them
iii.	Develop categories	Categories are developed from the data by open coding of the data
iv.	Saturate categories	Further examples are gathered as one proceeds through the transcripts until no new examples of a particular category emerge
v.	Abstract definitions	Once the categories have been saturated, formal definitions in terms of the properties and dimensions of each category may be generated
vi.	Theoretical sampling	From the categories which have emerged from the first sample of data, relevant samples are theoretically chosen to help test and develop categories further
vii.	Axial coding	Using the method of axial coding, possible relationships between categories are noted, and hypotheses are actually tested against the data obtained in ongoing theoretical sampling
viii.	Theoretical integration	A core category is identified and related to all the other subsidiary categories by means of coding, and links with established theory are made
ix.	Grounding theory	The emergent theory is grounded by returning to the data and validating it against actual segments of the text
x.	Filling the gaps	Finally, any missing detail is filled in by further collection of relevant data

Source: Bartlett and Payne (1997: 183).

Though data are initially considered to be free of theory, in that Glaser and Strauss originally recommended that the researcher should avoid presuppositions, other hypotheses and previous research studies, it is accepted that at some stage the emergent theory should be tested against theory developed by other researchers and should thus become part of the cumulative development of theory about society. Strauss and Corbin (1994: 227) have recently accepted that 'they (Glaser and Strauss) greatly underplayed ... the unquestionable fact (and advantage) that trained researchers are theoretically sensitized'. The original *tabula rasa* approach was heavily criticized (cf. Bulmer, 1979) on the grounds that researchers bring with them to the setting a mass of partially formed theories and ways of understanding the social world, which inevitably impact upon initial decisions about data-collection, the boundaries of the field being studied and the methods used. However, though they modified their position, their validity criteria are still whether the analysis is grounded in the data: i.e. monosemically formed from it. This implies three tests: comprehensiveness (the theory takes account of all the data); logical coherence (the one correct way of organizing and representing the data is identified and applied); and phenomenological bracketing (the analyst is able to put to one side his or her preconceptions and prejudices during the analysis).

This leads onto the second point about the processes described above: the inductive nature of their project. Clearly, grounded theorists accept that theory must always emerge from the data, though early theory is subsequently tested against later data; and, indeed, the emergent nature of theory means that both inductive and deductive processes are at work. Furthermore, the emergent theory drives later data-collection methods; thus grounded theory represents the relationship between data and theory as dialectical. At different moments the one drives the other and vice versa. The inductive strategy that this represents has been described by Harré (1972) as consisting of three principles. The first of these is the principle of accumulation. Scientific knowledge consists of a series of facts about the world and it grows by the addition of new facts, which do not affect the integrity of the old facts. The second principle is the principle of induction, whereby 'there is a form of inference of laws from the accumulated simple facts, so that from true statements describing observations and the results of experiments, true laws may be inferred' (ibid: 42). The third principle is that of instance confirmation, whereby a greater number of instances of an event being observed allows a greater degree of belief in the law.

Blaikie (1993) subsumes these three principles into a four-stage model: (1) all facts are observed and recorded without selection or guesses as to their relative importance; (2) these facts are analysed, compared and clustered, without using hypotheses; (3) from the analysis, generalizations are inductively drawn as to the relations between them; (4) these generalizations are subjected to further testing. The inductive strategy therefore suggests that the method for developing theory is logical and, furthermore, that there are regularities in nature which can be logged using the appropriate procedures.

DEDUCTION

Critical rationalists such as Karl Popper (1976) argue that we cannot make observations without invoking a theoretical schema of some sort; and that the induction process implied by inductivists, whereby theory-building always proceeds from the collection of observable facts, is flawed in both a logical and practical sense. His critique rests on the notion that because a number (however large) of similar events have occurred, then we cannot conclude that a causal relationship has been established. In other words, there are no logical grounds for extrapolating from past experiences to future occurrences. The classic example is the statement that all swans are white. This was assumed to be true until black swans were discovered in Australia. An illegitimate conclusion was drawn from a sequence of events: the observation that swans are white. In addition, because Popper accepted that all observations are theory-dependent, then necessarily there is a deductive element in social theorizing. Deductivists begin with implicit and explicit theories about the world which they then proceed to test in and on the world. The precise origin of these theories is left deliberately obscure: Popper professed no real interest in their genealogy. However, this testing can never provide absolute proof of the truth of an hypothesis or theory; repeated testing only allows both the rejection of clearly false theories and the development and refinement of others. In addition, if a theory cannot be potentially falsified, it cannot be considered a theory at all.

Popper (1976: 89–90) sets out his method: (1) The method of the social sciences consists of trying out tentative solutions to certain problems: the problems from which the investigations start, and those which turn up during it. Solutions are proposed and criticized. If a proposed solution is not open to pertinent criticism, then it is excluded as unscientific, although perhaps only temporarily. (2) If the attempted solution is open to pertinent criticism, then an attempt is made to refute it; for all criticism consists of attempts at refutation. (3) If an attempted solution is refuted through criticism, another attempt is made. (4) If it withstands criticism it is accepted temporarily; and accepted above all, as worthy of being discussed and criticized. (5) Thus this method of science is one of tentative attempts to solve problems, by conjectures which are controlled by severe criticism. It is a consciously critical development of the method of 'trial and error'.

Popper's solution depends on, though this is not explicitly stated in his writings, a distinction between knowing and being, or epistemology and ontology. Since the means of getting at the truth are always bound to be fallible and are immersed in specific time-bound traditions of knowledge (this is at the epistemological level), it is never possible to know reality as such (this is at the ontological level). Social scientists can in fact only make rational guesses about it and then test those guesses as best they can. However, since knowing is subject to changing conditions, to know absolutely is a fiction. Knowing, for Popper, does not have a teleological finesse about it; only by careful conjecture and refutation can theories be developed about both the natural and social worlds.

There are a number of problems with this approach. First, since all observations are theory-impregnated, the testing of theories against observations has a circularity about it. Thus when Popper rejects the notion of psychoanalysis as unscientific because it cannot in theory be falsified, the test itself is unfair because it assumes a particular configuration of observable data which is not shared by psychoanalysts. Second, the move from the critical deductive process to the rejection of theories if they cannot be potentially falsified does not follow logically. Popper is here making two separate points. Third, the rejection of a theory because it has been falsified rather than verified implies that reality can never be known as such. This is because his critical deductive approach never allows one to say that one theory is better than another because it accords with experience, but only that it might be a good theory because it has been modified as a result of being tested against the world of facts. This endless process of hypothesizing is ultimately self-defeating.

Popper's celebrated attack on inductivism and his advocacy of a deductive strategy, albeit one that has been considerably modified from traditional versions, points to the difference in approaches adopted by inductivists and deductivists. However, as we observed with a typical inductive approach such as grounded theory, there are elements of induction and deduction within it. A fairly typical deductive approach is as follows: (1) A research hypothesis is developed. This comprises the identification of a number of discrete variables which the hypothesis suggests co-exist in a specified way. (2) The hypothesis is operationalized, so that the relations between variables and the operation of the variables themselves can be construed as observational data and can be measured. (3) Data are collected and a strategy, whether it be experimental, survey or case study, is chosen. In addition, a sample of cases is made, and the relationship between this sample and its parent population established. (4) The empirical data are then used to confirm, disconfirm or partially confirm the original hypothesis or hypotheses. (5) This process may be replicated, and if this further process of testing is successful the hypothesis becomes accepted as theory.

Popper's modified version of deductivism nullifies one of the traditional criticisms made of this approach, which is that data can never be free of the preconceptions and frameworks of the data collector. However, more significantly, the method lacks predictive power because it is wholly based on events that occurred in the past. This is because it eschews the inductive principle of inferring from past occurrences to future events. Because neither inductive nor deductive research strategies have provided convincing explanations of how social scientists develop knowledge of society and educationalists of educational systems and activities, other strategies have been suggested: retroduction and abduction.

RETRODUCTION

A way of solving the problems created by induction and deduction has been suggested by critical or transcendental realists (cf. Bhaskar, 1979). Again, the first move that is made is to distinguish between the epistemological and the ontological realms (in fact, unless this is done, Bhaskar argues, theorists are guilty of the ontic fallacy – the unjustified conflation of these two levels). Those constant conjunctions or patterns of events that are experienced are merely the appearance of reality; they reflect real mechanisms that are causal in nature and that exist at the transcendental level and therefore do not make themselves immediately known. In fact, he posits three levels or domains: the real, the actual and the empirical. In the domain of the real resides the mechanisms, powers of which drive actual events that produce actual experiences. These events are real, whether they are observed or not. If they are, they are located in the empirical domain. A theory is realist, therefore, if it acknowledges that: (1) something is objective, in that it exists whether it is known or not; and, furthermore, it may still be real without appearing so; (2) all claims are fallible, in that they are always open to refutation and further exposure to the collection of data; (3) all claims to knowledge are transphenomenal – that which is real goes beyond and underlies appearances – these underlying mechanisms endure longer than their appearances and make them possible, indeed generate them; (4) finally, reality may actually be counter-phenomenal – in other words, knowledge of real structures certainly will go beyond appearances, but in addition may actually contradict appearances.

In order to achieve understanding, careful experimentation has to take place in order to actualize mechanisms. In other words, researchers can set up a situation in which the three domains coincide. Bhaskar (1979: 4) argues that

> we have in science a three-phase schema of development, in which in a continuing dialectic, science identifies a phenomenon (or range of phenomena), constructs explanations for it and empirically tests its explanations, leading to the identification of the generative mechanisms at work, which now becomes the phenomena to be explained, and so on. On this view of science, its essence lies in the move at any one level from manifest phenomena to the structures that generate them.

For Bhaskar, though this procedure more obviously applies in the natural sciences, a unity of method between the natural and social sciences is both possible and desirable.

The retroductive research strategy has been summarized by Blaikie (1993) following Harré (1961) and Keat and Urry (1975) as follows: (1) If the purpose of doing the research is to explain regularities between observable phenomena, then the task is essentially one of discovering those mechanisms and structures which underpin them. (2) These structures and mechanisms are not immediately available to consciousness and therefore the first stage of the process is to construct a possible model of them, drawing on evidence from what is observable. (3) Such modelling is an attempt to explain phenomena causally, i.e. these mechanisms and structures have causal properties. (4) The next stage is to test the model. However, this does not involve straightforward experimentation, because the conditions for the exercise of these causal powers may not be in existence. (5) If the testing is successful, this allows the researcher to believe or at least to have good grounds for believing in the existence of these structures and mechanisms. (6) The whole process may be repeated so that the existence of these structures and mechanisms is confirmed.

Clearly, the viability of such a method depends on a belief in realism, albeit of a sophisticated kind. It also depends on a conceptualization of reality which includes unobservable entities. The existence of these mechanisms and structures is inferred from a complicated process of experimentation and testing.

ABDUCTION

The abductive strategy is the one generally used by hermeneutic or interpretive researchers and focuses on drawing out the meanings used by social actors as they live their daily lives. The principle is best expressed by Giddens (1976: 161), when he suggests that 'the production and reproduction of society thus has to be treated as a skilled performance on the part of its members, not as merely a mechanical series of processes'. What follows from this is that 'we cannot describe social activity at all without knowing what its constituent actors know, tacitly as well as discursively' (Giddens, 1984: 336). This perspective gives due weight to the descriptions that actors provide of their intentions, plans and projects. To do otherwise would be to fall into the trap of conceptualizing the human actor as the 'unwitting dupe' of structural forces beyond their control and thus not able to act intentionally.

Three broad traditions have dominated sociological thought since its inception. The first focuses on the brute and imposing facticity of society and relegates the human actor to a subsidiary role. This may take the form of subservience to society as a functional whole (Parsons, 1964), to the overwhelming pressure exerted on the superstructure by economic arrangements (Marx, 1976) or to the constraining influence of discursive frames within which actors seek to make sense of their worlds (Fairclough, 1992). These forms of downward conflation between the cultural and sociocultural spheres provide little real evidence that human actors can control their destinies and are reflexive beings who monitor and thus by implication change their behaviours.

Pitted against this is a view which emphasizes the active and intentional flow of social life. Sociologists who work within this tradition recognize the central importance of the social actor in their descriptions of social life. More extreme versions ignore the pervasive and routinized character of much of that social life and seek to sustain a notion of *Verstehen* (Weber, 1964) without recourse to any constraining influences exerted by society. Such interpretive and interactive philosophies have found expression in movements such as symbolic interactionism, ethnomethodology and some forms of ethnography.

More recently there have been various attempts to provide a synthesis and in doing so give full weight to both structure and agency in social life. This points to one of the major weaknesses of interactionist and interpretive methodologies. The stress on descriptions of the intentions and plans of social actors fails to position and locate these activities within the enabling and constraining contexts of life. The emphasis is on the agential thrust of activity, with a consequent neglect of structural influences. The most compelling of the interpretive and meaning-based methodologies is symbolic interactionism, and much of the empirical literature in the field of the sociology of education over the past decade and a half has been influenced by it in one form or another.

Its founding father is G. H. Mead, an American social psychologist, who developed a perspective on the maturation of the self that became known as interactionism. He identified two stages in this development: play and game. Prior to this, the child, not being aware of the meaning of actions, is only able to imitate the actions of others. At the play stage, the child begins to experiment with role-playing, in particular assuming the roles of 'significant others'. Each role is compartmentalized and the child has little understanding of the relations between roles. The next stage, game-playing, is more complex. The child is now able to comprehend the totality of all the roles of all the players in a game situation. For Mead a game is simply a metaphor for any coherent and holistic social activity. However, the full development of the self involves an awareness that the group, community, or society as a whole 'exercises control over its individual members'.

The process by which this form of control is exercised is complicated and involves a division of the self into two parts, the 'I' and the 'Me'. The 'I' is an evolving phenomenon and can control and direct the self to act in an independent manner. The 'Me' is the way in which the self understands how it is seen by others. Fundamentally, it can be held up by the 'I' for inspection. Hargreaves (1972: 11) describes the effects of this conception of self:

> In Mead's analysis of the self, the individual becomes a kind of society in miniature, for he can engage in a form of internal social interaction. When, through the process of taking the role of the other, the self acquires its reflexive quality and attains selfconsciousness, the individual is no longer at the mercy of the forces of nature. He does not merely respond to those forces which play upon him from inside or outside, as is the case with objects or organisms that lack a self. In short, his behaviour is no longer directed. With a self, the self ceases to be subject to the direct impact of other stimuli, for he can withhold his response to such stimuli and estimate their significance and consequences for particular lines of action towards them. His ability to anticipate makes several possible future lines of action available in the present; and from such future possibilities he can make a choice. The person thus constructs and chooses what he does; his acts are not predetermined responses.

Two important concepts are central to interactionist analysis. The first is that of negotiated order: people negotiate the various roles they are expected to play. The second is that of interpretation. Roles, behaviour and understanding are dependent upon interpretive activity. The emphasis on the intentional aspect of human activity has been criticized because it involves a number of unwarranted assumptions about human behaviour and also fails to come to terms with societal constraints. Human beings are not equally able to control and influence events: society is stratified in various ways. This means that some human beings have greater degrees of freedom than others. Second, interactionism implies that society is simply the amalgam of a series of individual decisions, and cannot operate as a specific material constraint; a notion that is hard to sustain.

Symbolic interactionism leaves certain unanswered questions about epistemology; in particular, about whether researchers should attempt to maintain the integrity of the phenomena they are studying. Most theorists working from an interpretivist perspective accept 'that it is necessary for social scientists to grasp lay concepts of social actors, to penetrate hermeneutically the particular form of life; that social theories need to be built on everyday concepts' (Blaikie, 1993: 207). What is at issue is how far theorists and empirical researchers should go beyond this; in other words, whether the concepts and ideas used by the social scientist should be anchored in lay discourse or whether it is methodologically acceptable to import other notions which social actors may not recognize. This movement from first-order to second-order constructs involves abductive reasoning and may take a number of forms. Schutz (1963), for instance, describes it as a process of developing models of typical social actors, which by virtue of how they have been constructed have typical motives and behave in typical ways:

> Yet these models of actors are not human beings living within their biographical situation in the social world of everyday life. Strictly speaking they do not have any biography or any History, and the situation into which they are placed is not a situation defined by them but defined by their creator, the social scientist. (ibid: 339)

However, for him, these second-order constructs are always directly related to and anchored in lay descriptions of the social world. There is of course a sense in which the empirical researcher always goes beyond the self-constructed life-notions developed by participants. The process of collecting data is an intrusive act by the researcher; even in the course of an interview, the researcher's biography imposes an order on how the social actor understands their life. When this is inscribed in a text of some sort, a further process of intrusion takes place. The hermeneutic process always involves closure at some arbitrary point by the researcher. This closure takes the form of a 'going beyond' the way of understanding developed by the social actors under scrutiny. Abduction therefore comprises this movement from lay to technical accounts of social processes and lives, and is an alternative to inductive, deductive and retroductive strategies. Each of them needs to be understood in terms of the critique we have developed in Part One of this book; that is, these ways of thinking are embedded within epistemological and ontological frameworks which allow us as researchers to say some things and at the same time do not allow us to say other things.

PART TWO

Strategies and Methods

FIVE

The Experimental Method

In Part One, we referred to four different research paradigms: positivism, interpretivism, critical theory and postmodernism. In Part Two we move from paradigm to strategy, always conscious that the strategic level implicitly draws on epistemological and ontological understandings. Researchers take up particular positions in relation to these which guide their choice of strategy and ultimately method.

The experimental researcher attempts to explicate causal relationships between phenomena by intervening in the natural setting and controlling the relevant variables. A number of examples of the use of this method are given in this chapter: testing the effectiveness of a curriculum to increase AIDS awareness among year 8 pupils in a school; discovering whether a new method of geography teaching improves pupils' knowledge and understanding; and comparing different strategies for the teaching of reading. Three approaches have been developed. The first is where a single group of participants is tested before and after a programme of interventions to determine whether that programme has been successful or not. A variation on this is where a control group is added, so that comparisons can be made between it and the experimental group. The third approach is where the researcher accepts that more than one variable may be influential, arguing that a particular variable affects behaviour in one context, but not in another. In order to take account of this, the researcher studies a number of groups, each of which has different characteristics, and each of which is subjected to different types of interventions. Experimental researchers use methods which are essentially deductive, and involve the testing of hypotheses. Furthermore, such methods allow replication, and ultimately the establishment of law-like propositions about social activity. Experimental researchers would argue that as a result uncontested and secure propositions about the way in which society works can be established.

INTERNAL VALIDITY

Campbell and Stanley (1963) have identified two types of problems with experimental methods. The first type refers to the internal validity of the experiment. Can researchers be sure that the effects they ascribe to the interventions in their experiments are in fact caused by those interventions and not by other factors?

- *History*. Experimental subjects have other experiences during the timespan of the experiment, and the researcher may, as a result, mistakenly attribute such effects to the intervention.
- *Maturation*. In a similar way, can experimentalists be sure that the effects they attribute to the intervention were actually caused by it, and would not have occurred anyway due to the maturation of participants in their research?
- *Pre-test sensitization*. This refers to the ability of the tests to induce abnormal or artificial behaviours. It is conceivable that participants performed better than they normally would have during the intervention because they had been, and would subsequently be, tested.
- *Test reliability*. Theorists (Wood and Power, 1987) have argued that tests are imperfect instruments for measuring capability. They identify a gap between competence and performance, and they suggest two forms it might take: false negative and false positive. In the first instance, due to anxiety, test nerves and a host of other reasons, test-takers underperform. In the second instance, the test overrates their capabilities. False-negative cases are, of course, more common than false-positive ones. Furthermore, test indicators have to be precisely formulated. If the test is unreliable, it is difficult to be sure that the findings of the experiment show what they purport to. Furthermore, whether observations of behaviours or testing of attributes is undertaken, there is always the danger that changes occur in the testing routine before and after the intervention, and these constitute a possible form of bias.
- *Selection*. Experimental researchers who operate with control groups have to ensure that the experimental and control groups are as like as they possibly can be. Furthermore, both groups must remain intact throughout the duration of the project, especially if they have been chosen randomly. This tendency for members of the different groups to drop out is known as experimental mortality. Both effects – selection problems and experimental mortality – may have the consequence of decreasing the researcher's sense of certainty about the validity of their findings.

EXTERNAL VALIDITY

In contrast to internal validity, external validity refers to sampling procedures and to whether findings can be generalized to larger populations. Again, Campbell and

Stanley (1963) have suggested four areas of doubt concerning the ability to generalize findings. These are:

- The researcher's inability to conceptualize performance indicators, so that other researchers can replicate the experiment.
- The researcher's inability to ensure that their experimental and control groups are representative of larger populations.
- The researcher's inability to be confident that the way they operationalize variables in the experimental setting can be replicated in real-life situations.
- The researcher's inability to be certain that internal validity variables such as history, maturation, pre-test sensitization, test reliability and selection will not detrimentally affect external validity. If the former threaten the validity of the findings, then equally they threaten the ability to generalize to larger populations and other settings.

ONE-OFF CASE STUDY DESIGN

Here a group is exposed to some form of intervention and then subsequently tested. This design might be illustrated as shown in Figure 5.1.

Experimental group	Process observed or measured

Figure 5.1: One-off case study design

It has been described as lacking any form of control and therefore of being of no scientific value. The reason is that those factors which contribute to the internal invalidity of the findings are not controlled for. Other experiences may have contributed to the scores subsequently obtained, whereas the impression is given that they were caused by the experimental intervention. In a similar way, the effects of maturation, test reliability and selection have not been ruled out and could account for the improvement. This design has weak external validity, and generalized conclusions from the setting cannot be safely made. However, though there is an absence of control factors, the process of observing experimental interventions is common practice in much educational research and evaluation, and is underpinned by a different set of assumptions about how we can research and understand social reality.

SINGLE-GROUP EXPERIMENTAL RESEARCH

The least complicated version of this type of research is the single-group pre-test and post-test design. An example might be the implementation of a curriculum programme which has been devised to improve AIDS awareness among year 8 pupils in school. This consists of a week's intensive teaching, using interactive and didactic methods. Prior to its implementation, the pupils are tested about their knowledge of the effects of AIDS. After the intervention, the pupils are again tested. If a comparison between the scores on these two tests shows that these pupils now have more knowledge of AIDS, it is possible to conclude that the teaching programme has been successful in its aims. Diagrammatically, single-group experimental research can be shown as in Figure 5.2.

| Experimental group | Pre-test | Special treatment | Post-test |

Figure 5.2: Single-group experimental design

There are several problems with this approach. Tests do not always measure what is intended. In the example above, the tests may not have measured the actual level of AIDS awareness amongst the pupils both before and after the intervention. Tests, in other words, can be invalid. They can also be unreliable. Since the pre-test and the post-test have to be either the same or at least similar because the researcher intends to make comparisons between scores on the two tests, it is essential that pupils who sit the first test do not discuss their answers with other pupils. If they do, it is difficult to determine whether learning has taken place as a result of the testing process or teaching programme.

Experimental subjects cannot be isolated during the experiment, but continue to lead normal lives and are subject to a variety of other influences. Learning opportunities, besides those provided in the teaching programme, occur naturally; pupils, for example, may watch a television programme on AIDS. These may act as more significant influences on learning than the teaching programmes. As a result, it is difficult for the researcher to be sure about the source of any increase in AIDS awareness.

Furthermore, it is difficult to conceal from pupils that they are taking part in a special teaching programme, and this may affect their behaviour. They may concentrate better than they normally would because they know that they are going to be tested at the end of the programme. This is known as pre-test sensitization.

Finally, if the findings from the experiment are to be applied to all year 3 pupils in the country, then this creates a number of problems. Are these pupils typical? Do, in other words, they learn in similar ways to all other pupils of this age? It is well established that a large number of social factors affect learning: gender, class, race, affluence and so forth (cf. Burgess, 1986). Does the profile of this particular group of pupils fit the national profile? Is it legitimate to draw generalized conclusions from the sample? The answers to these questions determine the external validity of the findings.

THE STATIC GROUP COMPARISON

The third pre-experimental design identified by Campbell and Stanley (1963) introduces the notion of a comparison group. This is an attempt to isolate the effects of the experimental intervention, and to clearly distinguish between them and those other factors which may contribute to the results. If the control group when it is tested shows different results from the experimental group, then it is possible to conclude that the intervention has had an effect. This design may be illustrated as shown in Figure 5.3.

Intervention with the experimental group	Group tested
No intervention with the control group	Group tested

Figure 5.3: Static group comparison design

Researchers are comparing here the experiences of the control group during the experiment with the experiences of the experimental group. They may conclude that, if they are measuring, for example, reading ages as a result of a programme designed specifically to accelerate reading skills, the experiences of the control group, though not directly related to the intervention, have contributed to gains recorded on standardized reading tests. Once again with this design, because of the lack of controls, they may unjustifiably be attributing gains made on a reading test to the intervention when, for various reasons, those gains would have occurred anyway. They therefore cannot conclude that they have established a causal relationship between a programme and its effects in terms of increased skills amongst participants.

THE PRE-TEST POST-TEST CONTROL GROUP DESIGN

These types of design have been described as true experimental designs because they always include processes of randomization. As with the static group comparison design, it is important to be aware that the comparison which is made is not between a controlled intervention and nothing at all, but between two different types of experiences of two different groups, the one being planned and designed and the other being what would have happened anyway. The pre-test post-test control group design is shown in Figure 5.4.

Randomly picked experimental group	Pre-test	Special treatment	Post-test
Randomly picked control group	Pre-test	No special treatment	Post-test

Figure 5.4: Pre-test post-test control group design

Figure 5.5 shows an experimental design to discover whether a new method of geography teaching improves pupils' knowledge and understanding.

| Group A | Tested for geographical knowledge | Received new method | Post-test |
| Group B | Tested for geographical knowledge | Received old method | Post-test |

Figure 5.5: Pre-test post-test control group design illustration

Having conducted the experiment, the researcher collected and tabulated the data as shown in Table 5.1.

Table 5.1: Pre-test post-test control group design illustration

	Pre-test (average group scores)	Post-test (average group scores)	Improvement
Group A	48%	63%	15%
Group B	48%	53%	5%

There are a number of problems, even if the conclusion was drawn that the new method seemed to have increased pupils' knowledge and understanding. In order to be absolutely sure, it would be important to check that the two groups were similarly matched and that the conditions in which they were taught were the same.

A number of variables may have had an impact on how the old and new methods are received; for example, there may be a gender bias in one group compared with the other. If there is, is this a significant factor in the success or otherwise of the teaching programme? For the comparison between the scores obtained by the two groups to be valid, those other factors which may affect the amount and quality of learning have to be controlled for. Only then can the researcher be certain that the one method of geography teaching (Method A) is a better method than the other (Method B). If less time is spent on Method B, or Method B is always taught in the afternoon when the children are less attentive, or in poorly decorated and crowded conditions, then he or she cannot be certain that Group B has performed less well than Group A because of the type of teaching method being employed. A partial solution to this problem is afforded by the process of random sampling. If two groups can be picked randomly (the one to act as the experimental group and the other to act as a control group), then it is possible to be fairly certain that internal characteristics of the two groups will be similar. The effect of randomly choosing experimental and control groups is that members of each group have an equal chance of being influenced by factors other than the intervention.

However, there is a major problem, which is that randomization is difficult to achieve in certain social settings, especially when the researcher wishes to compare groups in schools which may have been picked so that they are deliberately not equal, i.e. with streaming. In other words, they come to a setting which is already determined beforehand and their interventions therefore relate to the teaching of those pre-determined groups. There is a similar problem with matching pairs or groups, which has been described as an alternative to randomization (cf. Moser and Kalton, 1977), in that in order to assign matched pairs to different groups and then to intervene at the group level, the researchers would have to be in a position to create new groups. In much social and educational research, this is simply not possible. There is a further problem with assigning students to matched pairs and this is that researchers have to be aware of, and confident in their ability or other people's ability to measure, those variables in order to identify appropriate subjects. In other words, they have to know before they do their research what those variables are to allow them to match one child with another.

A further variation of this design is when the experimentalist foregoes the pre-testing process and is confident that, having picked randomized groups, they will be equally matched. This is known as the post-test only randomized control group design. The reason for this is that measuring the abilities and aptitudes of subjects beforehand is irrelevant to the identification of equally alike groups since the experimentalist is concerned above all with the comparative effects of interventions. Equally, there are good reasons as to why it may not be possible to pre-test the various groups; for example, it may be inconvenient or not practically possible. However, the main advantage is that it eliminates the possibility of reactivity or pre-test sensitization to the experiment, thus enhancing its internal validity. Randomization allows the experimenter a measure of control over the setting which is properly denied to those designs which are known as quasi-experimental.

FACTORIAL DESIGN

As we have suggested, sometimes more than one variable is influential. In the example above, it was suggested that different groups of children may respond in a different way to the same teaching programme. If this turned out to be true, it would be important to take into consideration more than one variable – the intervention (in this case, a teaching programme) *and* the propensity of a group of pupils to respond in a particular way.

Experimental researchers have devised strategies for dealing with this problem. The following is an example which involves the teaching of reading. An experiment to test the effectiveness of Method A versus Method B in teaching reading proved inconclusive. However, the researcher hypothesized that Method A is better for below-average readers, and Method B is better for those who are above average. He or she was interested in conducting an experiment to test the relationship between method and ability. Four groups were identified (Figure 5.6).

Group 1	Pre-test reading ages	Method A – high ability	Post-test reading ages
Group 2	Pre-test reading ages	Method B – high ability	Post-test reading ages
Group 3	Pre-test reading ages	Method A – low ability	Post-test reading ages
Group 4	Pre-test reading ages	Method B – high ability	Post-test reading ages

Figure 5.6: Factorial design illustration

Data were collected by pre-testing and post-testing and compared (Table 5.2).

Table 5.2: Factorial design illustration

	Pre-test average scores	Post-test average scores	Improvement
Group 1	12.6	13.0	6 months
Group 2	11.9	12.9	12 months
Group 3	7.4	8.7	15 months
Group 4	7.8	8.0	4 months

Pupils were aged between 9 and 10.
Data were collected using a standardized reading test; figures here represent standardized reading ages.

It is possible to conclude that Method A is more appropriate for low-ability children than Method B and that Method B is more appropriate for high-ability children than Method A. One can go further and suggest that Method A is a better method for teaching reading to low-ability children than Method B is for teaching reading to high-ability children. However, it is also possible to conclude that these findings are problematic, because the experiment's internal and external validity is weak.

A different type of four-group design may also be used (Solomon, 1949). Here only one type of intervention is considered but it is treated in a number of different ways. The advantage of this is that the external validity or general-izability of the intervention effects is considerably improved. The design is as shown in Figure 5.7.

Randomized group A	Pre-test	Receives intervention	Post-test
Randomized group B	Pre-test	No intervention	Post-test
Randomized group C		Receives intervention	Post-test
Randomized group D		No intervention	Post-test

Figure 5.7: Four-group design

The effect of the intervention is replicated in four different ways. Experimentalists can compare pre-test and post-test scores with a single group (Group A) that has received the intervention. This will allow them to make a valid comparison but it may have weak internal and external validity. The second comparison they can make is between a group which has not been subject to the intervention (Group B) and one that has (Group A), though this does not allow them to filter out the effects of testing – both its potential unreliability and its potential reactivity. They can therefore determine the differential between scores achieved by Group A and Group B, when one has been subjected to the experimental intervention and the other has not.

The third comparison they can make is between Group C and Group D, where the former has only been tested after the intervention, while the latter has received no intervention but has been post-tested. This allows them to make a judgement about the effects of the intervention when test-sensitizing effects have been eliminated. The children could not have behaved in unnatural ways because they were being tested, though there may still be a problem with the sensitizing effects of the intervention itself. This has the effect of increasing the ability of researchers to generalize to other settings. Finally, they can compare Group C and Group B, where the former has been post-tested but not pre-tested, while the latter has been pre-tested and post-tested even though it has not been subject to any intervention. Again, this allows them to be more confident that the experimental mechanism which they have set in place is not responsible for the effects they observed and therefore allows them to be more confident about generalizing to other settings.

THE PROBLEM OF TIME

One of the main problems with conducting experiments is that the effects of an intervention may not show up, or the full implications of the intervention may be only partially revealed, at the moment of testing (post-testing). An example could be in the field of health education, where the experimenter is interested in testing for the effects of a smoking prevention programme, the intervention comprising a teaching programme with a group of 15-year-old schoolchildren. The intervention consists of lectures, seminars, workshops and written exercises. The aim is to reduce both the number of children who start smoking after the age of 15 and the number who have already started. Because smoking take-up is heavily influenced by peer group pressure, the effectiveness of any health promotion intervention is likely to be compromised. However, in later life, when the influence of the peer group has considerably declined, learning which took place at an early age, but which had no immediate effect in terms of smoking cessation, influences later decisions to stop smoking. In other words, the experimenter has to choose, in an arbitrary fashion, the most likely moment to post-test the children, even though he or she is fully aware that the observed effects may be partial, incomplete and possibly misleading. Experimentalists have therefore devised a series of designs to compensate for this, though that compensation can be only partially effective. One such design is shown in Figure 5.8, and is known as the time-series experiment.

$Test_1$	$Test_2$	$Test_3$	Intervention	$Test_4$	$Test_5$	$Test_6$

Figure 5.8: Time-series experimental design

Another is the equivalent time-samples design, in which a series (random or regular alternation) of interventions are consecutively contrasted (over time) with a series of non-interventions. This is usually a single-group design (Figure 5.9).

$Time_1$	Intervention and post-test
$Time_2$	Non-intervention and post-test
$Time_3$	Intervention and post-test
$Time_4$	Non-intervention and post-test
$Time_5$	Intervention and post-test
$Time_6$	etc.

Figure 5.9: Time-samples experimental design

Finally, there are what are called counter-balanced designs, where four different experimental treatments are compared using four different groups over four different time periods. It can be displayed as shown in Figure 5.10.

	Time$_1$	Time$_2$	Time$_3$	Time$_4$
Group A	Intervention$_1$ and post-test	Intervention$_2$ and post-test	Intervention$_3$ and post-test	Intervention$_4$ and post-test
Group B	Intervention$_2$ and post-test	Intervention$_4$ and post-test	Intervention$_1$ and post-test	Intervention$_3$ and post-test
Group C	Intervention$_3$ and post-test	Intervention$_1$ and post-test	Intervention$_4$ and post-test	Intervention$_2$ and post-test
Group D	Intervention$_4$ and post-test	Intervention$_3$ and post-test	Intervention$_2$ and post-test	Intervention$_1$ and post-test

Figure 5.10: Counter-balanced experimental design

INTERVENTIONS

As we move from examining randomized and controlled designs to quasi-experimental ones, we begin to incorporate a large number of designs that would not normally be thought of as fitting within the experimental tradition. Furthermore, these may involve deliberate interventions in the naturally occurring sequence of events and subsequent evaluations of their effects. For example, Scott *et al.* (1997) conducted an evaluation of the effects of a computerized programme to accelerate numeracy and literacy amongst 7-, 8- and 9-year-olds in English schools. The programme was made available to children and teachers in 15 schools in the Docklands area of London. Six hundred children were tested (using standardized reading and spelling tests) at three points in time: before the intervention, half-way through and at the end. No comparison groups were used and it was accepted that the groups in the 15 different schools which took part in the project were not equally constituted. That is, they differed in size, ability, home environments, class, wealth, etc. The main form of comparison here was not between the different groups but between the different school cohorts at different points in time; as a result, their progress could be observed in the 15 schools. This loose quasi-experimental design allowed a measure of comparison.

Indeed, we can take this argument one step further and argue that all research involves some form of artificiality. Life-history interviews, for example, have the effect of changing – by allowing the subjects the possibility of reconstructing past events in their lives – the nature of the reality being studied. However, they differ in some fundamental respects. No attempt is made to isolate a causal relationship by controlling through randomization and comparison. Indeed, the intervention itself and its effects are not the object of study. Furthermore, a close relationship is accepted between reality and the methods used to capture it; the purpose of the exercise is the reconstruction itself and not the representation through a controlled design of the underlying reality itself.

CRITIQUE OF THE EXPERIMENTAL METHOD

Though researchers working within psychology and related disciplines use experimental methods, in particular with regard to reading, such methods are not generally used by the educational research community. Some of the problems associated with such methods have already been referred to, and this gives us a clue as to the reasons for their apparent underuse. These problems are five-fold. First, effects may be more subtle or difficult to conceptualize than researchers allow for. This difficulty takes a number of forms. We have already referred to the time dimension of effects and the way these effects may not show up or may only partially show up at any one moment or series of moments. Further to this is the fact that those effects may be such that it is not possible to display them in quantifiable form; or at least, if they are displayed in this way, researchers are involved in a decontextualizing process in order for them to meet the two essential conditions for enquiry into closed systems – there must be no change in the object over a period of time and across different cases, and those external conditions which allow them to operate must remain constant. This is discussed in greater detail in Chapter 6. However, the point being made here is that for the variable to be operationalized, the experimentalist must be in a position to satisfy themselves that the construct being examined is the same across all the cases being studied, and that what is actually being examined reflects what is intended to be examined. If we take an example, this will bring out the force of the argument. Standardized reading ages refer to reading ability in a technical sense, i.e. as a measure of the ability of a child to decode the written text. What they do not do is measure the general level of competence of the child, the way in which the reading material impacts on the learning of the child, the way in which the text is understood by the child, the relations between these decoding processes and other forms of learning and so forth. Another example might be to do with truancy rates. If the notion of truancy is understood in different ways by different people and these different constructs are themselves a part of the reality being investigated, then the experimenter may have a problem with their need to operationalize such variables.

The second problem is related to this and refers to the inappropriateness of the use of such methods when researchers are dealing with those causal mechanisms which underpin social life. Here we assume a distinction between 'successionist' and 'generative' theories of causation, developed by Harré (1972). Successionist theorists, following Hume (1739), understand causation as beyond observation. Researchers can observe successive occurrences, but they can never capture the causal impulsion which connects them. The experimentalist operates by randomly allocating subjects to control and experimental groups and observing the differences. Causation, therefore, is external and non-observable, and the key is to distinguish between the causal relationship and any spurious associations. Generative theories of causation understand the process differently. Causation acts internally as well as externally. Causality describes the transformative potential of phenomena. One happening may well trigger another but only if it is in the right condition in the right circumstances. Unless explanation penetrates to these real underlying levels, it is deemed to be incomplete. (Pawson and Tilley, 1997: 34)

They go on to argue that: 'In pursuing causal explanation via a constant conjunction model, with its stress on that which can be observed and controlled, it has tended to overlook the liabilities, powers and potentialities of the programmes and subjects whose behaviour it seeks to explain' (ibid.). A number of points need to be emphasized here. First, if this is correct, then the methods of data-collection and the research design are going to be different. The reason for this is that researchers are now committed to understanding mechanisms which may not actually operate in practice (i.e. produce effects) because the external conditions for the release of the generative mechanism may not be present. They therefore have to adopt a two-fold strategy: identifying the appropriate generative mechanism and examining the actual conditions which have produced the effects that they have observed. Since the reality which they wish to describe is social in nature and thus comprises social actors interacting with each other, they cannot simply assume that those actors are compelled to behave in certain ways by causal mechanisms which they cannot observe. They should be understanding such causal relations as configurations of social actors making decisions, whether appropriate or not, within certain determinate conditions and that the making of those decisions changes both the contexts in which future decisions are made and the identity of those self-same social actors. Second, as we will suggest in Chapter 6, by employing different methods they are in a better position to distinguish between real and spurious causal relations, expressed as they are in terms of the constant conjunctions of events that the researchers observe.

We can go further than this and suggest that context is indeed the most important factor in understanding human relations and cannot be written out of the equation as 'mere noise'. One aspect of these contextual factors comprises the reasons that social actors give for their actions – the constructs by which they understand the nature of reality. This is never more obvious than with the question of race. Government statistics both describe and, more importantly, construct (though this is denied) racial configurations by collecting data in the way they do. An Afro-Caribbean category both includes and excludes by virtue of the fact that a person so designated may not actually understand themselves in any way as fitting such a category. The categorization itself is therefore an act of power and not merely a descriptive device by which governments and others can understand social life. Thus critics of experimental approaches argue that researchers need to understand both the contexts in which social actors exist and the contexts in which the data are collected; in short, the culture of the setting. For philosophers such as Giddens (1984), social phenomena cannot be understood without reference to the accounts given by participants in those social settings which are being examined. Those constructs developed by researchers may, and indeed in most cases do, have an impact on the constructs used by social actors, thus changing their nature. This renders the production of law-like statements about human activities problematic.

The fourth problem with experimental research in education is that of ecological validity. Can researchers generalize from the experimental case to other cases in time and place? If they can, the assumption is made that social actors behave in determinate ways – behaviours triggered by the intervention in one set of circumstances will be replicated in a similar set of circumstances elsewhere by a different set of social actors. There are two problems with this and they need to be distinguished. The first is that experimentalists construct settings which are deliberately artificial in character, and this may mean that firm conclusions about whether human beings actually behave like this in real life cannot safely be drawn. There is, however, a stronger argument. We are dealing here with a set of relations between structure and agency, which Archer (1988) describes as downward conflation – that is, the overwhelming power of structure reduces human beings to a malleability which denies them any sense of choice. Experimentalists make claims about human nature and the rules which structure behaviour which are reductionist in kind. For Archer (1982), structural relations provide good reasons for social actors to behave in certain ways, but they are never absolutely compelling.

Finally, we come to the ethical problem associated with experimental research and this is that it is discriminatory because one group of social actors is given preferential treatment, even if it is not known until the experiment has been completed which of the groups it is. This has been countered by suggesting that experimental treatments provide knowledge about human relations which can only benefit humankind in the long term. Thus an assumption is made that the subjects receiving the less successful treatment are denied treatments which would be of benefit to them for the sake of others both now and in the future. This suggests a view of educational research which is cumulative, rational and teleological. Such a view has been discussed in more detail in Part One. Suffice it here to suggest that the development of a nomothetic science of education is as yet unfulfilled.

SIX

Survey and Correlational Designs

A second, though not unrelated, strategy used by educational researchers comprises survey or correlational designs. The most common forms of these are based on a positivist epistemology and a naive realist ontology. Such a view has been criticized both from a transcendental realist position (this is made explicit in this chapter) and from a post-positivist, anti-realist position (see Chapter 2). In Chapter 2 we suggested that, though few would directly support a positivist viewpoint, it still remains influential as a set of intellectual resources. An example of a piece of research in this mode is discussed in the second part of this chapter.

Survey researchers collect data about larger populations than experimental researchers. Surveys may lead to simple frequency counts or to more complicated relational analysis. In educational research there are two important types. The first is correlational research, in which through the use of various statistical devices, relationships between phenomena are identified and a calculation of the probability of those relationships holding firm in other settings is made. The second is ex-post facto research, in which the researcher searches for causal relationships among phenomena by retrospectively reconstructing what happened. Data are collected in a variety of ways, and their collection typically involves structured interviews, postal questionnaires, standardized tests of performance or the use of attitude inventories. Surveys have one main advantage and this is that data are collected from a large number of respondents. In order to do this, the method, usually in the form of a questionnaire, is standardized. This means that respondents are expected to understand each question in the same way.

That they may not could be due to a number of common faults in questionnaire design, as follows:

- *Response overlap* – if the respondent is asked to choose from a set list of possible answers, those answers need to be mutually exclusive. If they are not, then response overlap occurs and this may cause confusion among respondents.
- *Imprecise questions* – the context or intended meaning of a question must be obvious to respondents; otherwise they are likely to understand it in different ways, which would mean that comparisons between these different answers could not be made.
- *Complexity* – if a number of questions are condensed into one, this may provide several sorts of information at once, but it is likely to lead to confusion amongst the respondents.
- *Awkward phrasing* – an example might be the use of double negatives, which again may lead to confusion among respondents.
- *Overprecise questions* – an assumption is made that the respondent can give precise information, when in these cases only imprecise information is available.
- *Composite questions* – each question needs to be distinct so that only one type of information is being elicited. If composite questions are included, then during analysis it is difficult to separate out the different responses.
- *Elaborated questions* – if the question is too complicated, then it may need to be explained to the respondent. Though this is possible with interview surveys, standardization of response may be put at risk.

Questionnaires are constructed in a number of different ways, using different types of questions, as follows:

- *Simple closed factual questions* – coding occurs before fieldwork, and the assumption is made that the respondent will give a yes or no answer.
- *Simple open factual questions* – coding occurs after fieldwork because all the possible answers are not obvious to the researcher.
- *Structured factual question* – coding takes place before fieldwork, and respondents are offered a number of discrete choices.
- *Simple closed opinion questions* – coding takes place before fieldwork, and respondents are offered a number of different options which are presumed to cover all the eventualities.
- *Closed structured opinion questions* – these types of question follow on from simple closed opinion questions, but attempt to elicit a larger amount of information.
- *Simple open opinion questions* – these are post-coded and usually take the form of how or why questions.
- *Closed structured statement banks* – these include banks of statements which respondents choose between.
- *Open description* – this type of question allows the respondent the space to develop their answer without obvious restrictions.

- *Open lists* – respondents are asked to compile lists of advantages and disadvantages of particular courses of action.
- *Closed list or checklist* – respondents are asked to indicate how they feel about the topic and are provided with a list of items.
- *Structured rank order lists* – respondents are asked to place a list of items in rank order of importance for them.
- *Open rank order list* – respondents are asked to make a list in rank order of a preference.
- *Partial agreement statement or question* – respondents are asked to state their own degree of agreement or disagreement with a statement or in answer to a question.
- *Partial agreement oppositional constructs* – respondents are asked to state their own degree of agreement between sets of oppositional constructs.

These types of questions differ in two fundamental respects. Possible answers to questions are either determined beforehand, or the questions themselves are open and respondents are given the opportunity to express their feelings and opinions and to provide information in as full a way as they can. The second distinction is the way in which their answers are treated. The restriction of respondents to a set of pre-determined answers involves a number of assumptions: that the data will be treated quantitatively and thus compared in a standardized way; and that all the possible responses to the questions are determined beforehand and made available. On the other hand, if the question type is open-ended, this preserves the possibility of the data being treated either quantitatively or qualitatively. Coding can, as a result, either conform to the dictates of statistical modelling or be understood thematically. Though qualitative researchers generally use semi-structured interviews and observations to collect their data, they also make use of diaries and other written records. The open-ended questionnaire may serve the same purpose, though ethnographers are now dealing with a larger number of cases than they normally would.

SAMPLING

Since survey researchers are concerned with large populations and they may not be in a position to survey all the members of their population, they can sample that population. There are two principal types: probability and non-probability surveys. In the first case, criteria for selecting respondents are known; in the second case, the criteria are unknown. Probability sampling allows probabilistic generalizations which are always expressed with indices of error. Error is more likely to occur with smaller samples. However, increasing the sample size does not produce exponential gains in accuracy. Furthermore, the greater the variability in a population and the more complicated the analysis that is intended to be made, the larger the sample size has to be. Probability sampling may be conducted in a number of ways (cf. Robson, 1993).

- *Simple random sampling* – this is where the sample of a population is selected randomly. The randomization principle allows the researcher to be certain that each member of a population has an equal chance of being selected. It is important to note here that, though it is likely to produce a representative sample (especially if the sample size is large), the mean of a stratified sample in certain circumstances may be closer to the mean of the population (this happens when there is limited variability in the characteristic being considered).
- *Systematic sampling* – this is a variation on randomization, where the population is divided into strata or groups of respondents who share a common characteristic. Each stratum is then randomly sampled. This may lead to either proportionate sampling, where the relative numbers in each group reflect the actual numbers in the population as a whole, or disproportionate sampling, where there is unequal weighting. This latter may be desirable when some characteristic of a group needs to be emphasized because of the focus of the research.
- *Cluster sampling* – this comprises the selection of clusters which contain individuals who comprise the object of study. The cluster may be chosen on a random basis, with individuals within each cluster then being sampled as a whole.
- *Multi-stage sampling* – this comprises various levels or stages of sampling so that, for example, education systems are sampled; schools within those chosen systems are then randomly chosen; classes within these schools are randomly selected for study; and, indeed, within each class, children may then be randomly sampled for detailed investigation.

In most cases it is not possible to select probability samples, especially where the relevant characteristics are not known in advance. Generalization from the sample to the population is therefore more difficult to make, except in those cases where the researcher is confident that the whole population is included in their sample. This is quite common, e.g. all student teachers studying physical education in the Hong Kong Institute of Education. Non-probability sampling comprises a number of different strategies (cf. Robson, 1993):

- *Quota sampling* – an attempt is made to make the sample represent as closely as possible the characteristics of the population being surveyed, though it should be emphasized that the identification of the characteristics of the population is made before the survey is carried out. The research itself is likely to furnish more information about the population which may cast doubt on the representativeness of the sample actually chosen.
- *Dimensional sampling* – here researchers make sure that their sample contains examples of individuals with specific characteristics which are thought (or which have been established by pilot work) to be relevant to the focus of the study.
- *Convenience sampling* – this comprises choosing an unrepresentative sample by

selecting respondents because it is convenient for the researcher. This method is frequently used by the media when they want to take a snapshot of opinion about a particular issue.

- *Purposive or theoretical sampling* – this type of sampling is much used in case study work, where the design is considered to be emergent. Sampling decisions within the case are made in terms of the developing theory. Thus sampling and theory are understood as dialectical and symbiotic.
- *Snowball sampling* – this consists of the researcher identifying gatekeepers to a particular setting, who then act as guides or informants about the appropriateness of further sampling within the case.
- *Time sampling* – individuals may be studied across time or in terms of a particular sequence of activities within which they have a central role.
- *Extreme case sampling* – the purpose of this type of sampling is to focus on unrepresentative and extreme cases of particular activities or behaviours. This is common in case study work.

STATISTICAL PROCESSES

This book is not intended to be a primer on statistical method; rather, it attempts to understand the ontological, epistemological and methodological implications of different research strategies. However, some discussion of statistical approaches is necessary. Heyes *et al.* (1993: 3–4) define statistics as 'describing the world in terms of numbers and making evaluations and predictions based on those descriptions'. The essential building block is the variable, and this is defined as 'any property or characteristic of some event, object or person that may have different values at different times depending on the conditions' (Pagano, 1990: 5–6). There are two types of treatment. The first is descriptive statistics, in which the intention is to summarize the data or present them. There are a number of ways of doing this. Frequency tables are simple counts of instances of a variable and these may be expressed as tables (usually expressed as number and as percentage), bar charts (the height of each bar shows its value or frequency), pie-charts (the angle from the centre is proportional to the frequency), histograms (these express continuous data in bar form and are useful for expressing relative frequencies of the data set), frequency polygons (joining together the mid-points of the bars of a histogram) and scatter plots (these express on a graph the relationship between two different variables). The numerical or quantitative data collected from observations, interviews or questionnaires may be nominal (counting), ordinal (ranking) or interval (measuring differences). Descriptive statistics are also used to show the distribution of the data set, which may be unimodal (single variable), bimodal (involving two variables) or multimodal (more than two variables). Most distribution calculations depend on their relation to a notional idea of a normal curve or shape. Distributions, therefore, may be normal, skewed to the right (positive) or to the left (negative), and either flat, bell-shaped or thin (kurtosis). Various statistical devices are used to measure the arithmetic mean, median, mode or standard deviation of a particular data set, and these are set out in many standard textbooks and in Bryant and Jones (1995).

The second type of statistical treatment is inferential. This goes beyond merely describing the data. Bryant and Jones (1995: 5) give four purposes:

- to draw conclusions from the data obtained from a given sample of research subjects about the population as a whole from which the sample has been drawn.
- to determine whether the statistical results produced by the research could or could not have been achieved by chance. If not, then the results can be said to be significant; if so, then the results can be said to be not significant.
- to determine the level of confidence in the significance of research results.
- to test hypotheses about relationships between variables.

These relationships are known as correlations, and are defined as a measure of the extent to which an increase or decrease in the value of one variable is accompanied by an increase or decrease in the value of another variable. The principal way of calculating this is by measuring the correlation coefficient, and this is expressed as $+1$ (a perfect positive relationship has been established between two sets of variables), -1 (a perfect negative relationship has been established between the two sets of variables), 0 (no relationship at all between the two variables) or a score between $+1$ and -1. However, it needs to be emphasized that any correlation established does not imply the existence of a causal relationship, but may suggest it. Furthermore, correlations only enable researchers to make predictions within certain determinate limits.

More advanced statistical techniques can be used to allow the researcher to make predictions about the relationship between two or more variables. These techniques are known as regression procedures. The simplest is linear regression analysis, which is sometimes called the line of best fit. The idea of regression is to plot a line on a graph that best explains the relationship between two variables and then infer from the line instances of that relationship which go beyond the data that have been collected. A more accurate expression of this can be determined by a mathematical equation known as the regression coefficient. Non-linear regression techniques are suitable for determining the line of best fit between two variables which do not operate in a linear fashion; multiple regression techniques are appropriate for determining the predictive relationship between more than two variables. A research project that has made use of these techniques is discussed below.

'SCHOOL MATTERS: THE JUNIOR YEARS'

An example of a study using the techniques discussed in this chapter is an investigation into the effectiveness of schooling in a sample of junior schools in the London area (Mortimore *et al.*, 1988). The study had four main purposes: first, to develop a detailed description of pupil and teacher activities and of how the schools organized themselves and their curriculum; second, to document the progress of the children in the schools (the cohort numbered nearly 2000 children); third, to determine whether and how some schools were more effective than others in promoting the learning and development of their pupils; and fourth, to investigate whether the different characteristics of pupils had any effect on the children's progress and development.

Three categories of information were collected: pupil intake data in terms of schools, classes and individuals; educational outcomes of pupils, classes and schools; and classroom and school environmental data. Background measures of pupils' characteristics comprised social, ethnic, language and family data, and initial achievement data at entry to junior school. This was a longitudinal study and an analysis was made of the cumulative effects of these background factors during the course of the study. Cumulative data were also collected about each child's attainment in reading, mathematics and visio-spatial skills. The purpose of collecting such data was to assess each child's progress when pre-school and other influences were accounted for. Such baseline data allow a measure of the progress and development of each individual child to be made.

The second type of information that was collected comprised measures of educational outcomes. The research team collected data about cognitive outcomes using standardized tests of reading and mathematics at frequent moments during the project. In addition, individually based assessments of practical mathematics and creative writing were made at yearly intervals; oral skills of a sample of the children at the end of their fourth year were assessed; and data from the Authority-wide pre-secondary transfer tests of reading and verbal reasoning were collected. The study also collected data on non-cognitive outcomes. This comprised information about children's behaviour in school. In addition, pupils' attitudes towards different types of school activities and the curriculum by self-reporting were examined. Children were asked to assess how they were seen by their teacher and peer group at the end of their third year, and full attendance data were collected for each child at regular moments during the project.

The third type of information comprised data about the classroom and school environment. Each headteacher and deputy headteacher was interviewed about the way in which the school was organized. Class teachers were questioned about their qualifications, responsibilities, philosophies and involvement in decision-making. Detailed information about their pedagogic strategies, special needs teaching, implementation of the curriculum and use of timetables was also collected. Classroom observations, using pre-set tick-box schedules, were made in each of the three years. In addition, 'extensive use was made of qualitative data, including notes, case studies and verbatim descriptions provided by the field officers' (ibid: 6). Parents of a sample of pupils were interviewed. Finally, a wide variety of methods was used to collect data about the pupils, classes, teaching staff and schools in the project. The reason for collecting such a wide range of information was not only to be comprehensive, but also to allow cross-checking between different accounts.

Three aspects of the effects of junior schools on their pupils were examined in detail:

- The size of the effects, in terms of the proportion of the overall variation in pupils' progress or development which can be explained (in a statistical sense) by different schools, in comparison to that explained by the children's background characteristics.
- The size of the effects of individual schools on their pupils' educational outcomes. (For example, what difference in a pupil's reading progress over three years can be attributed to her or his membership of a particular school?)
- The processes which relate to the effects of individual schools and classes on their pupils' educational outcomes. (ibid: 7)

A multilevel modelling process was used to assess these effects both across the three years of the project and within each year, and this enabled the separate effects of school and class to be identified and studied. In addition, data on individual attainments by pupils for differences due to age, social class, sex and race were collected. The mathematical modelling which took place allowed separate investigation of these different factors, when all other background factors were eliminated from the analysis, and examination of progress and attainment for children with different characteristics (i.e. age, social class, sex and race).

From this description of the project, a number of conclusions can be drawn about methodology and research strategy:

- Though a blend of quantitative and qualitative data were collected, the general focus of the project was on the creation of a mathematical model to explain certain school effects.
- The design of the research was pre-determined and not emergent.
- The intention was to collect associational data, and then to infer from them causal relationships.
- The population was defined as London primary schools and it was suggested that the final list of factors related to these schools.
- Though the project team comprised a number of research officers, attempts were made to standardize data-collection procedures between the different schools. This was to allow proper comparisons to be made.

- The project's intention was to discover patterns of events or their constant conjunctions.
- The values, preconceptions and epistemological frameworks of the research team were considered irrelevant to the design of the research, or, at least, they were not reported as considerations.

We need to examine these and other constructs, in particular with regard to school effectiveness projects of recent origin.

MATHEMATICAL MODELLING

School effectiveness researchers (Creemens and Scheerens, 1989; Levine, 1992; Mortimore *et al.* 1988) have in recent years made a number of claims about education systems. Their thesis is that individual schools make a difference to the relative achievements of children regardless of the socio-economic conditions in which those schools operate. For example, Smith and Tomlinson (1989: 301) argue that there are 'very important differences between urban comprehensive schools' in terms of the progress made by their pupils: 'the findings show that the same child would get a CSE grade 3 in English at one school, but an 'O' level grade B in English at another. There are equally large differences in maths and in exam results in total across all subjects.' They employ a methodology which involves the application of mathematical models to various complicated social processes. This allows them to separate out the effects of a number of variables thought to have an impact and to calculate the residual. This is defined as the school effectiveness quotient or that which is added by the school as a result of teaching and learning processes. Mortimore (1992: 32) argues that 'we define an effective school broadly as one in which students progress further than might be expected from consideration of its intake' – pupils are only being effectively educated if their achievements go beyond what would normally be expected of them.

This mathematical modelling of schooling measures performance in a standardized way – to allow comparisons between individual pupils in different settings. Furthermore, modellers choose those attributes that can be more easily quantified (i.e. reading ages as they are measured on a standardized test) or that have already been quantified (i.e. GCSE, Key Stage Tests or 'A'-level scores). Researchers in this field therefore take up a value position from the outset, and this contributes to their definition of effectiveness.

Performance is emphasized, and this is performance of a kind which can be reliably quantified. However, these measurements refer to performance at a certain point in time and in controlled conditions and not to the levels of competence reached by the child. Wood and Power (1987) distinguish between performance and competence (Table 6.1) and develop this distinction along two axes. The first relates to performance in the test situation – whether the child is successful or unsuccessful at the task. The second axis refers to what the child can

Table 6.1: Error types in relating performance to competence

	Success on task	Failure on task
Child has underlying competence (in sufficient degree)	Performance correlated with competence	False-negative error: failure due to factor other than lack of competence
Child does not have underlying competence (in sufficient degree)	False-positive error: success due to factor other than competence	Performance correlated with competence

Source: Wood and Power (1987).

do. Thus two types of error may result – false negative and false positive – and these occur because of the gap between competence and performance.

This can be illustrated by reference to recent evidence regarding the improvement in the performance of girls at GCSE and 'A' level in relation to the performance of boys (cf. Elwood, 1996). One possible explanation is that since the examination technology was changed (i.e. by the introduction of coursework in the GCSE and to some extent at 'A' level), girls are now better able to express what they can do, though Elwood (ibid: 300) suggests that this is not 'the sole explanatory factor'. Girls' underachievements in the past therefore related in part to the way they performed in test situations (i.e. as a result of the test technology) and not to their general levels of competence. However, it is impossible to separate these two factors in any meaningful way. This is so for two reasons: first, the levels of performance achieved by children influence what and how they learn and therefore affect the competence levels they achieve at a later point in time; and second, the gap between competence and performance for individual children varies and cannot be measured. If it is suggested that a more accurate expression of competence could be obtained by repeated testing and repeated measurement, this cannot solve the problem, since for some children it is those factors, inherent in the testing process itself, which sustain the gap between performance and competence. False-negative errors in testing make reference to an ideal which can be inferred but not quantified. If it could, then it would be possible to argue that, with a more sophisticated testing technology, the gap between competence and performance could be eliminated. Researchers could then be certain that a child's performance accurately reflects what he or she is able to do. Hammersley (1992) distinguishes between different meanings of the word 'accuracy' when he argues that precision or accuracy may not be best expressed quantitatively. Accurate descriptions of phenomena depend on their relation to the objects to which they refer and not to their ability to be expressed in mathematical form.

It is possible to go beyond this and suggest that the distinction between competence and performance referred to above implies a particular way of understanding this relationship and is therefore a theory-laden concept. Vygotsky

(1978) argues that a more useful notion of performance does not refer to the ability of the child to operate in standardized conditions but to the ability of that child to perform in conditions which maximize performance, and this of course might include collaboration between child and adult/teacher/tester. This refers to the zone of proximal development: competence is here being defined as the capability of the child to progress to higher levels of learning. Gipps (1994) characterizes this as a form of educational description and contrasts it with psychometric testing. It therefore cannot be measured, for a number of reasons: best rather than typical performances are examined; it takes place in relatively uncontrolled conditions; and it is essentially ipsative and thus seeks to make comparisons between different performances of the child rather than between performances of different children. This would suggest that standardized approaches to the collection of data used by school effectiveness researchers imply a theory about assessment and do not simply measure what is.

So one problem which has been identified is that, though school effectiveness researchers claim to describe what the school adds onto the learning of the child and that some schools add on more than others because they apply certain pedagogical and organizational principles to the process of schooling, in fact what they are referring to is performance on a narrow range of tests. Schools may be able to improve performance by the adoption of certain measures but this does not necessarily relate to learning: to what the child is able to do. Indeed, a school might be adept at improving performance, i.e. the ability to take a test, without being skilled at accelerating learning. It could be argued that each pupil in each school has an equal chance of performing well and that, therefore, even if competence cannot be measured, performance reflects competence in a straightforward linear fashion, but we have already suggested that this is not so. This is because those factors which mediate between competence and performance are variables which differ between schools, e.g. gender – girls perform better in certain types of testing situations than others (Gipps and Murphy, 1995).

A second problem with using test scores concerns the reliability of the marking of such tests. Nuttall (1987: 111) reminds us that 'research evidence suggests that the margin of error in a candidate's grade at 'O' level or CSE is about one grade in every direction'. Again, it can be argued that if researchers compare school with school, each school has the same chance of marking error with regard to their scores and therefore the comparison is still valid. However, if multilevel modelling techniques are used, as in many school effectiveness research projects (cf. Goldstein, 1987), with their reliance on data gathered at the individual level and from matched pairs of children, this matching becomes suspect.

One kind of variable has been examined and a number of problems with it identified. These are, of course, methodological problems, though undoubtedly they have implications for epistemology: that is, the methods researchers choose to enable them to understand phenomena in the world impact on the way in which they conceptualize these phenomena. However, the other set of variables used by school effectiveness researchers also needs to be examined. Levine (1992), for example, argues that schools which are unusually effective in value-added terms show the following characteristics: productive school climate and culture; focus on student acquisition of central learning skills; appropriate monitoring of student progress; practice-oriented staff development at the school site; outstanding leadership; salient parent involvement; effective instructional arrangements and implementation; and high operationalized expectations and requirements for students. In a similar way, Sammons *et al.* (1995) suggest that the following 11 interdependent factors are significant: professional leadership; shared vision and goals; an orderly and attractive working environment; concentration on teaching and learning; purposeful teaching; high expectations; positive reinforcement; monitoring progress; pupil rights and responsibilities; home–school partnership; school-based staff development.

CURRICULUM

There is a marked absence of curriculum factors. This de-emphasis of what should be taught in schools separates out curriculum from pedagogic and organizational concerns. A school could be an effective school regardless of what it teaches and what values it inculcates into its pupils. This separation of content from pedagogy is underpinned by a behavioural objectives model of curriculum design and a technical-rationalist view of pedagogy. In the first case, schooling is understood as a linear process which starts with the development of clear objectives or goals, proceeds through to the selection of content which is specified in behavioural terms – i.e. its acquisition must be an observable or testable process – and finishes with the evaluation of that process to see if those objectives have been met. As Tyler (1949: 3) puts it:

> if an educational program is to be planned and if efforts for continued improvement are to be made, it is very necessary to have a conception of the goals that are being aimed at. These educational objectives become the criteria by which materials are selected, content is outlined, instructional procedures are developed and tests and examinations prepared.

In the second case, it implies a particular model of teaching behaviour. If research is understood as the development of propositions about educational activities which reflect the world as it is, allow predictions about future educational states, and can be replicated by other educational researchers (cf. Levine, 1992; Sammons *et al.*, 1995), then this provides support for the technical-rationality model of the relationship between theory and practice. Here we refer to a model which conceptualizes the practitioner as a technician whose role is to implement 'objective' educational truths, and who therefore has a passive role in the implementation process. If it is possible to identify such 'truths' about education, the practitioner who chooses to ignore them is likely to make inadequate judgements about how they should proceed in practice. This is regardless of the need for practitioners to own or incorporate such findings into their own understandings to inform their practice (Rudduck, 1991). If theory about education which transcends context can be developed, then practice is better informed by it. The epistemological basis of the research methodology adopted and the development of lists of qualities to which educational practitioners are expected to conform reinforces this way of thinking.

This can be contrasted with process-orientated models of curriculum design and deliberative discourses of teacher behaviour (cf. Walsh, 1993). The behavioural objectives model has been criticized (cf. Stenhouse, 1975; Elliott, 1983) for the following reasons. First, complex and important learning outcomes of any educational programme may be neglected at the expense of the more trivial and less important, because it is easier to describe them in behavioural objective terms. Second, the pre-specification of behavioural goals may encourage an inflexibility of approach within the classroom, and learning outcomes that may incidently flow from classroom interaction will be deliberately underexploited. Third, there is a danger of assuming that if something cannot be measured, then it cannot be assessed and therefore it should not be a part of the learning process. Fourth, lists of intended behaviours do not adequately represent the way in which we learn: this is because logical order cannot be conflated with pedagogic process. McClaren (1995: 41) puts it in the following way: 'knowledge cannot be theoretically abstracted from its own production as part of a pedagogical encounter'. Equally, the technical-rationality model has been criticized because it seeks to treat teachers as technicians, whose role is simply to follow sets of pre-ordained specifications. In contrast, the deliberative is defined as those behaviours which lead to wise actions. It is therefore concerned with practical theorizing, and can only be judged to have succeeded by whether it has contributed to improved practice. However, the point is not to debate these various issues, but to suggest that what is seemingly unproblematic is in fact underpinned by a theoretical position, an epistemological stance, a particular understanding of theory and practice, and a conceptualization of the relationship between the two. In short, different approaches to researching schools will reflect different positions on these important issues (cf. Carr and Kemmis, 1986; Walsh, 1993; Scott and Usher, 1996), and the separation of facts and values which forms the centrepiece of our ideal model of positivism (see Chapter 2) is difficult to sustain.

CAUSAL RELATIONS

Two further issues need to be addressed in relation to these specifications of desirable behaviours. The first concerns the implicit unilinear model of causation subscribed to by school effectiveness researchers. Educational practice may be conceived of as deliberative action designed to achieve certain ends. What this implies is that there may be a number of different ways which are equally appropriate to achieve those ends. Indeed, educational subjects may respond in different ways to different pedagogic and organizational routines. However, the use of mathematical models to describe educational settings and the production of lists of specified behaviours would suggest a unilinear approach to school effectiveness. Quantitative modelling necessarily leads to certain ways of understanding schools and precludes others.

The second issue concerns the relationship between correlations and causal mechanisms. Even if a correlation can be established between two variables, it is still not possible to assert, in an unproblematic way, that the one caused the other to happen. There is always the possibility of a third variable causing variance in both. Furthermore, we cannot be sure which variable is prior to the other. Sanday (1990), for example, examines the first finding of a study by Mortimore *et al.* (1988) into effectiveness criteria in primary schools. He asks three questions, as follows. Does the observed correlation between the effective school (as identified by a battery of achievement tests conducted on its pupils) and purposeful leadership by the headteacher indicate that an effective school has to have this characteristic? Can a school function effectively without such leadership? Even if the headteacher does show purposeful leadership, could the school still be ineffective? Correlations are literally no more than this, and need to be distinguished from causal relationships.

Bhaskar (1979) makes a distinction between epistemology and ontology, in which he argues that epistemology is always transitive and therefore by definition substantially a product of prevailing power arrangements in society, but that ontology, certainly with regard to the human sciences, is relatively enduring and thus has a degree of intransitivity about it. Bhaskar needs to make this distinction to sustain his attack on positivism and its insistence on the atheoretical nature of data, and to cement in place his version of transcendental realism, which can be characterized in four ways: there are objective truths, whether they are known or not; knowledge is fallible because any claim to knowledge may be open to refutation; there are transphenomenalist truths in which we may only have knowledge of what appears and this refers to underlying structures which are not easily apprehendable; and, most important, there are counter-phenomenalist truths for which those deep structures may actually contradict or be in conflict with their appearances.

We have already suggested that regularities between phenomena that produce correlations cannot in themselves uncover causes. If the assumption is made that they can, then researchers fall victim to what Bhaskar (1979) describes as the ontic fallacy, the unjustified conflation of the epistemological and ontological realms. We can see this most obviously in some well-known examples. A hooter in London signalling the end of the day's work in a factory does not cause workers in Birmingham to pack up and go home, even if the two phenomena correlate perfectly over a period of time. A good correlation has been discovered between the human birth rate and the number of storks in different regions of Sweden, but the one does not cause the other to happen. The reason why these do not show causal relations and can therefore be described as spurious correlations is that the regularities so produced do not relate in a straightforward manner to the causal mechanism which produced them. One of the reasons for this is, as Bhaskar argues above, that deep structures may actually have contradictory appearances. But, more importantly, the way in which they have been expressed, i.e. in mathematical form, is an inappropriate way to describe them. Mathematics is an acausal system and can give us indications of causal relationships but never exact descriptions. However, ironically, the very precision demanded by the use of quantitative methods acts as a barrier to our determining whether our descriptions of causal mechanisms are accurate or inaccurate.

If the causal mechanism (this is an ontological matter) being described is to be perfectly aligned with the regularities observed (this is an epistemological matter), then we have a closed system. Science has been so successful because it has either created closed systems (i.e. much chemical/physical research) or been able to operate in closed systems (i.e. astronomy). For a closed system to operate, researchers have to be certain of two conditions. First, the mechanism itself must remain coherent and consistently so; that is, there is no change in the object over a period of time. Bhaskar calls this 'the instrinsic condition for closure'. Second, the relationship between the causal mechanism and those external conditions that allow it to operate must remain constant. If teachers in a school come to believe that democratic forms of management are inappropriate, then the effectiveness of those forms of management is likely to decline. The external conditions for the effectiveness of democratic systems have changed because one of them was a belief in democracy, and thus the system can no longer be thought of and treated as a closed system.

What are the implications of this? The most important one is that predictions about future states cannot be made with any degree of conviction from open systems. This is so because of the double hermeneutic involved in all social research. Human beings both generate and are in turn influenced by social scientific descriptions of social processes. There is, though, a second and more fundamental sense given to the notion of the double hermeneutic. Human beings, as reflexive and intentional actors, are engaged in interpretive activity throughout their lives. Symbolic interactionists argue that it takes a particular form: social actors come to see the world as others see it and to see themselves as others see them. They are thus able to reflect on, and reflexively monitor, their own actions. However, the presence of the researcher, and the researcher's desire to investigate social reality by focusing on the perceptions and behaviours of social actors, require a further level of interpretation. Researchers, therefore, interpret through their own conceptual and perceptual lens the interpretations made by those they are studying. The double hermeneutic involved in this determines the types of closure that can be made when researchers describe social reality.

Mathematical modellers of school processes, however, attempt to create closed systems of a different kind. The attempt at quantification always involves a series of reductive moves during the research process. Here we need to introduce the idea of two competing systems of thought. The first is the extensional idiom, and this is the system used by mathematicians. Standard logic attends only to matters of literal truth or falseness; that is, it is concerned only with the statement's extension. This implies that scientific description cannot concern itself with the intentions, beliefs and propositional attitudes of social actors; in short, that the intentional idiom is illegitimate. This belief, and this would point to its self-refuting character (Wilson, 1990), has underpinned mathematical, physical and chemical science research programmes and indeed much work in behaviourism, sociobiology and psychology. However, if it is accepted that social actors are conceptually different from inanimate objects, this creates certain problems in the application of mathematical models. As Wilson (1990: 398–9) points out,

> it is crucially important here to note explicitly that use of a mathematical model does not imply that descriptions are untainted by intention. Rather when researchers develop and apply such a model they arrange to package intentional idioms in such a way that, for the purpose at hand, they can proceed with formal calculations.

Researchers can do this in a number of ways, and in doing so they always proceed using the principles of additivity, linearity and proportional variation, and they make the assumption that objects to be compared over time (and the time factor is crucial when they are dealing with regularities) are invariant in their properties. Otherwise they are measuring different phenomena. If, on the other hand, the logic of the intensional idiom is that human activity is context-dependent, then it is harder for them to be certain that they are comparing like with like. That is, as Wilson (1990) points out, they make certain compromises with the data as soon as they use methods whose sole purpose is to allow them to quantify. These compromises involve the use of deductive techniques (as in much experimental work), the use of pre-set instruments (i.e. Likert scales in questionnaires) which determine and frame the types of answers they get as researchers, and the use of statistical techniques to analyse the data.

It is not so much that the types of closure occasioned by these techniques and by the use of these instruments is not parallelled in qualitative research, but rather that these forms of closure are determined beforehand to allow the development of mathematical models and therefore do not allow actors' descriptions of social life ever to be faithfully reflected in their research accounts. As Giddens (1984) argues, the production of models has to proceed from descriptions of social life by the actors involved, and researchers have to do everything they can to allow social actors to deliver to them authentic accounts of their lives. It has been argued that, if the researcher wants to investigate structural arrangements in society, then survey methods are usually considered to be the most appropriate. If that same researcher now wants to investigate a cultural setting, then he or she is more likely to use ethnographic methods. However, this gives a false picture. Giddens (1984), for example, suggests that social structures only have substance, and then only fleetingly, in the reasons agents have for their behaviours. He is therefore arguing that data which refer to the knowledgeability of agents are essential elements in social research, whether such study is of a macro-, meso- or micro-type. Methods which prevent the researcher from gathering reliable and valid data about this are not, therefore, appropriate or useful.

Giddens (1984) further elucidates four levels of social research. The first is the hermeneutic elucidation of the frame of meaning of the social actor(s) involved, the second is the investigation of context and the form of practical consciousness, the third is the identification of the bounds of knowledgeability, and the fourth is the specification of institutional orders. His argument is that quantitative researchers either pay insufficient attention to the first or collect data about it in the wrong order or ignore it altogether. What this schema also implies is that a purely phenomenological perspective is inadequate. This is so for four reasons: first, social actors operate within unacknowledged conditions, i.e. societal structures within which the actor is positioned; second, there are unintended consequences of his or her actions; third, social actors operate through tacit knowledge which is hidden by virtue of what it is; fourth, the social actor may be influenced by unconscious motivation. What this points to is the inevitable objectification involved in social research (i.e. the going beyond the purely phenomenological perspective) (cf. Bhaskar, 1989). However, as Giddens argues, this going beyond, in order for the explanation to be valid, has to involve an understanding of the perspectives of social actors, and the implication of this is that methods have to be appropriated which do not distort those meanings. There is therefore always an ethnographic moment in social research and this cannot legitimately be written out by quantitative researchers. It is with this in mind that we now turn to examining different approaches to the analysis of qualitative data.

SEVEN

Qualitative Research Design, Case Study and Theory-building

A number of approaches to theory development in educational research have been developed, e.g. statistical inference, where a sample of all the cases which constitute a population is identified and conclusions drawn from a detailed study of the sample are then deemed to apply to the population as a whole. This relationship is understood as probabilistic: any inferences about the population are made with the understanding that their accuracy is subject to statistical limits. This is contrasted with logical inference, where researchers make statements about the confidence they have that 'the theoretically necessary or logical connection among the features observed in the sample pertain also to the general population' (Mitchell, 1983: 207). Logical inference is defined as 'the logical relationship between' categories, when this relationship 'is not based upon the representativeness of the sample and therefore upon its typicality, but rather upon the plausibility or upon the logicality of the nexus between the two [or more] characteristics' (ibid: 198). These two positions represent different ways of understanding and developing theory.

A typical qualitative analytical approach may include the following:

- Coding or classifying field notes, observations or interview transcripts by either inferring from the words being examined what is significant (this is based on the way in which the case is being understood or on the developing theory), or from the repeated use of words or phrases which indicate that a pattern is developing (i.e. that all the activities which have been recorded are being understood in a similar way).
- Examining these classifications to identify relationships between them, and at

the same time beginning the process of understanding those relationships in general terms, so that they have credibility beyond the boundaries of the case being examined. Researchers draw upon previous knowledge about the world which has enabled them to distinguish between objects and between occurrences in their life.

- Making explicit these patterns, commonalities and differences – in short, making sense of the data, and taking these by now more developed theoretical constructs into the field to test or refine them.
- Elaborating a set of generalizations which suggest that certain relationships hold firm in the setting being examined, and affirming that these cover all the known eventualities in the data set.
- Formalizing these theoretical constructs and making inferences from them to other cases in place and time. This, in a sense, is the most problematic part of the procedure, because 'the basic problem in the use of case material in theoretical analysis ... is the extent to which the analyst is justified in generalising from a single instance of an event which may be – and probably is – unique' (ibid: 189).

Three processes are implied by this procedure: data reduction, data display and conclusion drawing and verification (Miles and Huberman, 1984). Data reduction refers to the process of simplifying the data so that they are manageable, or sampling from the data set by including what is relevant and excluding what is extraneous. As we suggested above, this includes those processes which occur before data-collection is embarked upon: choosing cases, sampling within each case, deciding on appropriate methods and so forth. All of these involve data reduction or focusing on one aspect of the setting at the expense of others.

Data display refers to the way in which those data are organized. This may include the use of matrices, graphs, charts, networks, flow diagrams and typologies. They are designed to compress the large amount of data into manageable form. The third formal procedure is conclusion drawing and verification. This is a more theoretically advanced stage and is concerned with the noting of regularities, patterns, explanations, causal relations, configurations and propositions. It may also involve the researcher in checking the validity of the theory which has been developed. Two principles guide this aspect of the work: the first is that the theory is internally credible – logical contradictions have been eliminated – and the second is that it is grounded in the data, or at least faithful to it. The theory that has been developed reflects the fieldwork in some logical and holistic way.

LOGICAL INFERENCE

We need to return to the distinction we made at the beginning of the chapter between statistical and logical inference. Mitchell (1983), in a well-known article, argues the case for a specific rationale for qualitative data analysis, and he goes on to suggest that this is distinct from the rationale adopted by quantitative researchers. His argument is as follows:

- Case studies are made, not with the intention of itemizing the features of a case, but in order to support theoretical conclusions: 'As a working definition we may characterise a case study as a detailed examination of an event (or series of events) which the analyst believes exhibits (or exhibit) the operation of some identified general theoretical principle' (ibid: 192).
- Within this broad general definition, there are five different ways of using case study material: *configurative-ideographic studies* (descriptions of the contexts surrounding events); *disciplined-configurative studies* (patterns of elements expressed in theoretical terms); *heuristic case studies* (the case is deliberately chosen to develop theoretical propositions); *plausibility probes* (testing the viability of pursuing rigorous testing of theoretical formulations); and *crucial case studies* (testing or falsifying a theoretical proposition) (Eckstein, 1975).
- Statistical inference comprises the identification of a representative sample when the characteristics of the parent population are reflected in those of the sample. This may be achieved by either random or stratified sampling. The certainty that a researcher is entitled to have is circumscribed by a notion of probability.
- Two problems arise. The first is that the characteristics of the parent population have to be known in advance if a representative sample is to be identified, especially if it is stratified; and the second is that an assumption is made about a particular type of relationship between characteristics: 'Note, however, that the inference from the sample in relation to the parent population is simply about the concomitant variation of two characteristics' (Mitchell, 1983: 198). It is not about the logical connectedness of those characteristics, i.e. the way in which they are actually conjoined in society. An example may serve to illustrate this point. A correlation is established between the age of teachers and their adoption of particular attitudes towards the introduction of a major government initiative such as the National Curriculum in the UK. In order for the researcher to understand the connection between the two, they have to resort to logical inference, i.e. that older teachers, having successfully established routines of work that meet their criteria for good teaching, are reluctant to change their practice, especially if they do not understand the rationale for change. Mitchell therefore argues that the success of this type of thinking depends not on the representativeness of the sample, but on the 'plausibility' or 'logicality' of the connection which is subsequently made.
- The relationship between the case and the wider population is therefore determined by whether the explanation derived by the researcher makes logical sense in terms of some systematic explanatory schema. The selection of the case is made not in terms of its typicality or even of its untypicality (since this is still operating within the logic of what is typical), but in terms of its explanatory power.

- Generalization from the case being studied to other cases in place and time therefore always involves prediction, though, for the reasons discussed in Part One, the predictive element as it applies to the future may be a special case. The predictive power of the case study is based on those necessary relations established in the case by a process of logical inference.

A number of problems with Mitchell's notion of logical inference and with the distinction he makes between logical and statistical inference come to mind. First, Mitchell is making an assumption that the population to which he refers is logically ordered in some specific way; that social actors behave in rational ways; and that the results of their interactions with other people produce orderly configurations. Furthermore, these may be known by examination of cases through a process of apprehending their logicality, i.e. the necessary relations which exist between different phenomena. He is therefore making the assumption that the world is an orderly place and conforms to the dictates of logic.

Second, Mitchell assumes that the boundary definitions that researchers make to connect the case with its parent population (albeit that they share the same logical nexus) are sound; indeed, that what enables researchers to make the connection is the sharing of a similar form of patterning. However, there is a circularity about the argument because the researcher is attempting to establish the viability of a connection between population and sample whilst at the same time assuming that it exists. If the distinction between logical and statistical inference is not entirely convincing, different ways of distinguishing between case study and other forms of research need to be examined. One argument is that there are sufficient significant epistemological and ontological differences between the two to justify their designation as separate forms of research.

CASE STUDY

Case study can be understood in two incommensurable ways: either as a set of procedures integral to all types of research; or as a paradigmatically separate form of research. Hammersley (1992) argues from the first of these two positions and does so by making a comparison between three strategies – ethnography, survey and experimental research. He concludes that each of these types of research utilize the concept of a case but treats it differently. Ethnographers, for example, choose to study particular segments of social life that are naturally occurring and that seem to have clearly defined boundaries, e.g. activities within a school over a determined time period. Though social actors within these boundaries also have experiences outside them, the boundaries are well enough understood to constitute the object of enquiry as a 'case'. Methods of data-collection are used that attempt to capture the 'lived reality' of such settings, and though these methods are usually referred to as 'qualitative', i.e. semi-structured interviews, observations of processes and documentary analysis, they are not exclusively so. Ethnographers, like Hammersley, therefore argue that the detailed description of the case that emerges can be complemented by examination of other cases that seem to have similar properties, i.e. other schools of a similar nature. Theory development is either cumulative, in that as more and more cases are studied, the database becomes more extensive and rich and the findings more reliable, enabling the researcher to generalize to larger populations, or theory developed from one or more cases can then be tested as to its validity and reliability by examining further cases.

Survey researchers, on the other hand, understand the 'case' in a similar way, but focus initially on a specified population. That is, they choose to concentrate on a group of seemingly like cases, e.g. all secondary schools in a locality or country, and work backwards so that the case is defined by the characteristics of the parent population as it is presently understood. Because the emphasis is placed on the examination of a large number of cases, each of them has to be conceptualized in a particular way; that is, the variables associated with them have to be understood similarly by participants and the assumption is made that these understandings correspond across the large number of cases. Furthermore, because the design focuses on a large number of cases and because survey researchers wish to compare such cases, then mathematical models are considered appropriate and these variables have to be expressed so that they conform to the principles of additivity, linearity and proportional variation. However, the important point to note is that the case is still being treated in the same way as in ethnographic research but with less attention to detail, context and presentation. The implication of this is that different methods are appropriate in survey research because researchers have to handle a large number of cases which, for the sake of comparison, have to be expressed in a standardized way. Thus survey researchers will typically use structured interviews, postal questionnaires, standardized tests of performance or attitude inventories. Furthermore, because the relationship between the case and the parent population is crucial, sampling decisions assume more importance. Cohen and Manion (1989) refer to two general methods of sampling. The first is probability sampling, in which the criteria for selecting respondents are known. The second, non-probability sampling, refers to criteria which are unknown. In the first instance, sampling may be systematic or stratified. In the second instance, sampling is less systematic, with the result that researchers can be less than sure that their sample of cases represents the larger whole about which they want to draw conclusions.

The other major implication is that there is a trade-off between detail and the ability to generalize. Hammersley (1992: 186) puts it in the following way: 'the choice of case study involves buying greater detail and likely accuracy of information about particular cases at the cost of being less able to make effective generalizations to a larger population of cases'. Thus, the difference between the two is not of kind but a matter of degree. If resources allowed, ethnographers could examine, using their familiar methods, a large number of cases which, when it reached a certain level, would be considered to be a survey; furthermore, the more cases they studied, the more confident they would be that their findings referred to all the possible cases in the field.

The second comparison Hammersley (1992) makes is between case studies and experiments, and here he once again argues that these designs are not fundamentally different but only different in degree, in this case the degree of artificiality. He suggests that

> the case study provides us with information that is less likely to be affected by reactivity and therefore is more likely to be ecologically valid; but it does so at the cost of making it more difficult to come to convincing conclusions about the existence of the causal relationship in which we are interested. (ibid: 192)

The trade-off here is between generalizability and the valid uncovering of causal relationships. In Chapter 5, we discussed the problem of explicating causality if experimental designs are used. However, Hammersley's argument is that experimental, survey and case study researchers complement each other. The complement comprises working at different levels of the educational system and should not be seen as in some way producing different and conflicting types of truth about what is being studied. This seems to be a coherent argument against the idea of epistemological paradigms as they impact on educational research.

Yet problems remain. For instance, Gillborn and Gipps (1996) suggest that in the field of educational research about race, different strategies produce conflicting truths. They cite evidence from numerous surveys about the incidence of racial prejudice among schoolteachers in the UK and suggest that these do not indicate any unacceptable level of racial prejudice and discrimination among the population surveyed. However, they then contrast this with frequent accounts by ethnographers/case study researchers which conclude the opposite. Here we have a major problem of validity. There are a number of explanations:

- The ethnographer's work, being unreliable, unstandardized and unplanned, simply reflects the intentions and unconscious biases of researchers, who, coming from critical perspectives, conclude what they wanted to conclude. Furthermore, the more rigorous nature of survey work allows these conscious and unconscious biases to be eliminated.
- Because the ethnographer can only study a small number of cases, sampling decisions are made that are more likely to confirm the implicit biases of the researcher, and thus it is not safe to generalize from such cases.
- The standardized methods employed by survey researchers are more easily manipulated by respondents, with the result that the survey researcher fails to capture the reality of life in schools. Semi-structured interviews, close and detailed observations of processes, respondent validation procedures and so forth rigorously eliminate these forms of distortion and produce a more valid portrayal of what is actually going on. The need to standardize acts as a barrier to the adoption of reflexive processes that allow valid accounts to emerge.

- The practical difficulties of collecting valid data about controversial aspects of school life mean that compromises with the data-collection are made, which means in turn that the findings from the various surveys are unreliable.
- Both types of researcher are unconsciously and implicitly operating from different epistemological and ontological perspectives and are therefore bound to produce different and in this case conflicting 'truths'.

If this is so, then Hammersley's argument that there are not three different paradigms at play in his discussion of experimental, survey and ethnographic perspectives needs to be examined further. Before we do this, it is worth looking at another distinction that has dominated methodological discussion over the last thirty years: this is the distinction between qualitative and quantitative approaches to research.

QUALITY/QUANTITY

This debate has been ongoing and fierce for much of the last thirty years, with different commentators arguing: that there is a need to resolve the underlying assumptions made by both sides (cf. Bhaskar, 1989); that we should move beyond the duality inherent in the distinction (cf. Hammersley, 1992); that a multi-layered approach should be adopted, whereby 'the use of quantitative data and forms of measurement' should be encouraged 'in order to complement the central core of qualitative analysis' (Layder, 1993: 127); or even that a resolution has occurred which has left those believing that it is a meaningful distinction 'on the outer fringes of the methodological debate' (Sammons et al., 1997: 8).

A way of resolving this apparent conflict has been proposed by Layder (1993), and this rests on the assumption that social explanation can operate at different levels of social life, and therefore different research strategies are appropriate for examination of each explanatory layer. It is to these arguments that we now turn. In the last chapter we made reference to Giddens's explication of four levels of social research. To reiterate, these are: the meaning frames of social actors; contextual features as they are understood by participants; the identification of the knowledgeability of these social actors; and the specification of institutional orders. For Giddens, the research process prioritizes the first three of these over the last, and this is because he wants to argue that social structures and institutional orders only have substance, and then only fleetingly, in the reasons that actors have for their behaviours. As we will see in Chapter 10, this duality has been criticized for tying agency and structure too closely together. Layder (1993) suggests a different typology, even if it has a similar purpose. He argues that research needs to apprehend the 'textured or interwoven nature of different levels and dimensions of social life' (ibid: 7). These different levels comprise: the self,

Table 7.1: Research map (adapted from Layder, 1993: 8)

Cohering element	Research element	Research focus
History	Context	Macro social forms (e.g. class, gender, ethnic relations)
History	Setting	immediate environment of social activity (schools, families, etc.)
History	Situated activity	Dynamics of face-to-face interaction
History	Self	Biographical experience and social involvement

situated activity, setting, context and history (this last applies to all the others). Table 7.1 illustrates the distinctions he makes.

His approach is therefore to argue that examination of each level is necessary for a proper understanding of the research setting, and that as a result qualitative approaches cannot be prioritized over quantitative approaches and vice versa.

Hammersley's (1993) position is different, in that he suggests that a number of false dichotomies exist, which if dissolved would render the distinction between quantitative and qualitative research redundant. These dichotomies are as follows:

- *Artificial settings/real settings* – quantitative researchers work in artificial settings such as laboratories or construct artificial situations to examine human behaviour; qualitative researchers work in real-life settings.
- *Precise description/general description* – quantitative researchers use precisely delineated categories; qualitative researchers make general descriptions of reality.
- *Focus on behaviour/focus on meaning* – quantitative researchers concentrate on social behaviours; qualitative researchers examine the meanings that social actors give to their activities.
- *Natural science/social science* – quantitative researchers believe that there is one correct method for understanding both the natural and social worlds; qualitative researchers believe that the social world is constructed in such a way that different methods are appropriate for each.
- *Deductive strategies/inductive strategies* – quantitative researchers use deductive strategies; qualitative researchers use inductive strategies.
- *Nomothetic statements/ideographic statements* – quantitative researchers develop nomothetic statements about the world; qualitative researchers acknowledge the uniqueness of social events and occurrences.

- *Realism/idealism* – quantitative researchers are philosophical realists; qualitative researchers are philosophical idealists.
- *Extensional idiom/intensional idiom* (not referred to by Hammersley (1993)) – quantitative researchers employ methods that treat the data as extensional; qualitative researchers employ methods that preserve the intensional integrity of the data.

Even a cursory glance at these dichotomies shows that, in most cases, a series of straw men have been set up. Ethnographers, for example, frequently collect data in artificial settings, may focus on behaviour as well as on meanings, may employ both inductive and deductive strategies, and so forth. However, there are two distinctions between quantitative and qualitative approaches that are far from chimerical. The first of these refers to the last item on the list and is discussed in detail in Chapter 6. To briefly reiterate, quantitative researchers are not able to deal with the intentions, beliefs and propositional attitudes of social actors. If they try to, they are engaged in processes of reification, packaging and ultimately distortion. This suggests that data-collection processes which do not involve quantification will have to be employed to fully understand the nature of the social world.

The second argument is more complicated. It suggests that there is a necessary relationship between the four levels at which researchers operate – method, strategy, epistemology and ontology – and that the quantitative–qualitative distinction can be shown to be inappropriate when applied at the first two levels, but to be significant at the levels of epistemology and ontology. Methods have been described as quantitative or qualitative, so that, in the former case, they comprise structured observational approaches, pre-set interview schedules, standardized tests, attitude inventories, and questionnaires. These can be contrasted with typical qualitative methods, i.e. semi-structured interviews and observations, or participant observation. This distinction assumes unjustifiably that quantitative instruments cannot be used to collect data that can then be analysed in a qualitative way. If we accept that they can, we have to conclude that it is not the instrument itself that determines the strategy but the way in which it is employed: a questionnaire has to be used in a certain way before the strategy can be considered to be quantitative, i.e. the questions have to be piloted, pre-set and capable of being understood in the same way by all the respondents. It is not the instrument itself, which is after all simply a device for collecting information, which designates the strategy as qualitative or quantitative. Indeed, participant observers use simple enumerative techniques in their work.

The next level is the strategic one, and it is here that the differences become more obvious. Typical quantitative strategies include experimentation, survey and ex-post facto designs. The design or strategy places a constraint on how the instrument is used. For example, if an experimental approach is adopted, then the data-collection instrument has to be pre-set and standardized to allow quantification. However, experimentation may in turn be understood in a number of different ways. If the experimental strategy is designed to compare randomly chosen experimental groups with control groups to allow a judgement to be made about the effects of an intervention, then the instrument has to be standardized and, moreover, a number of epistemological assumptions are made about the construction of knowledge, i.e. that the values, preconceptions and beliefs of the data collector do not enter into the collection of the data. If, on the other hand, the researcher is comparing observations before and after an intervention, then this does not prescribe a particular observer–participant relationship. The difference is made by the epistemological assumptions that underlie the strategy being used. These include: the relationship between the observer and the observed, the type of reactivity which is accepted, and so forth. What is being suggested here is that the epistemological and ontological relations within which the researcher is positioned drive the choice of strategy and method; and, indeed, that if the distinction between quantity and quality is to be useful, then it has to make reference to epistemology and ontology, and not just to strategy and method. It is to this that we now turn.

EPISTEMOLOGY AND ONTOLOGY

In order to sustain this argument, we need to make reference to the field of evaluation (the arguments against this being a separate activity from research are set out in Chapter 12). Simons (1988) refers to alternative approaches to traditional and largely experimental perspectives. These include: illuminative evaluation (Partlett and Hamilton, 1972); democratic evaluation (MacDonald, 1974); responsive evaluation (Stake, 1975); evaluation of literary criticism (Kelly, 1975); transactional evaluation (Rippey, 1973); educational connoisseurship (Eisner, 1975); and quasi-legal evaluation (Wolf, 1974). The important question to ask is whether these different approaches to evaluation actually comprise different epistemological and ontological viewpoints; in other words, whether case study, as it is defined by these different evaluation theorists, constitutes a different way of understanding how we can know the world (the epistemological dimension) and ultimately of what it is (the ontological dimension). Guba and Lincoln (1981) argue that case study work operates within a naturalistic perspective and is qualitatively different from experimental enquiry, which is underpinned by a set of scientific criteria that make certain assumptions about reality, the inquirer–subject relationship and the nature of truth statements (Simons, 1988). These differences are expressed by Guba and Lincoln in tabular form (Table 7.2).

Table 7.2: Scientific and naturalistic paradigms

	Paradigm	
Assumptions about	Scientific	Naturalistic
Reality	Singular	Multiple
	Convergent	Divergent
	Fragmentable	Inter-related
Inquirer (and relationship with subject)	Independent	Inter-related
Nature of truth statements	Generalizations	Working hypotheses
	Nomothetic statements	Ideographic statements
	Focus on similarities	Focus on differences

Source: Guba and Lincoln (1981: 57).

THREE TRADITIONS

Guba and Lincoln's first dimension is ontological, and Table 7.2 expresses different ideas about the nature of reality. The second is epistemological and again expresses different ways by which researchers can know that reality. The third dimension refers to the results of enquiries and the status of the claims that researchers make. There are three principal positions which can be taken in relation to these debates. Naive objectivism, or the belief that our conceptualizations about the world do not depend in some way on the theories we bring to it, has a long history and, though generally accepted by philosophers as misleading, still retains considerable influence in applied social science disciplines such as education. What is being invoked here is a separation of theory and fact, so that the facts speak for themselves. We are therefore led to believe that educational disputes can be settled by recourse to empirical enquiry, which consists of the collection of data about the world that represent it in some unproblematic way. The implication of this is that the researcher's values, conceptualizations and knowledge frameworks should not (though they frequently do) enter into the collection of data. Truth is therefore understood as free of those relations that characterize human activities – value disputes, differential orderings of roles, stratified positionings and the like. Indeed, power is carefully separated from truth (Mortimore and Sammons, 1997), with the consequence that use of the correct method will lead inevitably to an accurate statement about what the world is like. Furthermore, this is not an aspiration, as with Habermas's ideal speech situation, but a real possibility. Human frailty and fraudulent behaviour may mean that a distorted version of the truth emerges. However, what is being suggested is that a method has been discovered that guarantees us access to reality.

This can be contrasted with a belief in radical relativism, whereby observational data are never considered to be theory-neutral, but always mediated through structures, paradigms and world-views. Furthermore, these latter are not just epistemological frameworks but normative beliefs about how researchers would like the world to be. The implication of this is that no one framework is superior to another and that we simply have to live with such value disagreements. The way in which we therefore settle disputes is practical, by the exercise of power, whereby those with greater control of allocative (material features of the environment and the means of material production and reproduction) and authoritative (the organization of time–space, the body and life-chances in society) resources (Giddens, 1984) impose their view on the world. This results in various forms of idealism that imply a radical conjoining of thought and reality. Indeed, it challenges the distinction between statements and referents and implies that statements only refer to other statements and not to any underlying reality. This can be contrasted with the doctrine of naive objectivism referred to above, which signifies another conflation of thought and reality, but this time of a different nature. Sayer (1992: 47), for instance, argues that

> the illusion of the appeal to facts in popular discourse involves collapsing statements into their referents, thought objects into real objects. It thereby appears to appeal to the facts themselves, the way the world is, in an unmediated fashion, but it is actually an appeal to a particular way of talking about the world in some conceptual system, and therefore may be contested.

Whereas naive objectivism collapses description of the world into what it refers to, radical relativism does the same but in reverse order, collapsing reality into text.

There are a number of middle positions which do not involve conflations of these two. One such is transcendental realism, developed by Bhaskar (1989) amongst others. This was referred to in Chapter 6, and a distinction was made between ontology (being) and epistemology (knowing), so that to conflate the two becomes illegitimate – the ontic fallacy. Epistemology is always transitive, and therefore subject to the prevailing power arrangements in society. Ontology, certainly with regard to the social sciences, is relatively enduring. However, the relationship between the two is far from straightforward. To reiterate, he identifies four foundational principles: there are objective truths whether they are known or not; knowledge is fallible because any claim to knowledge may be open to refutation; there are transphenomenalist truths in which one may only have knowledge of what appears and this refers to underlying structures which are not easily apprehended; and most importantly, there are counter-phenomenalist truths in which those deep structures may actually contradict or be in conflict with their appearances.

There are a number of implications of this. First, we may actually be deceived by appearances. So, the constant conjunctions of events which we observe do not necessarily lead to the uncovering of causes. We should not confuse correlations with causal relations. Second, method is never unproblematic, but always involves an awareness that it is situated in time and place and therefore subject to particular arrangements of power. This means that values are central to the act of research – both the values of the researcher and the values of those being researched.

Another middle position is that taken by Alistair Macintyre (1988). He is anti-cartesian: Descartes (1949) argued that there are a number of foundational principles, that there is a logical way of proceeding, and that therefore it is possible to build systems of knowledge on firm foundations. Macintyre rejects this. Traditions of knowledge may share beliefs, images and texts; but what they do not have in common is criteria according to which participants arrive at practical conclusions about how to live, or 'practical rationality questions' as Macintyre calls them. They may come to an agreement to give a certain authority to logic, but what they agree upon is insufficient to resolve their disagreements.

Macintyre defends himself against charges that he is a relativist or a perspectivist. He argues that he cannot be accused of either of these because he rejects universal notions of rational discourse. The relativist challenge is that there are no rational standards. Every set of standards has as much or as little claim to our allegiance as any other. Perspectivists, on the other hand, argue that rival traditions are mutually exclusive, but do provide different but complementary perspectives on reality.

He suggests that these two positions and the naive rationalist position, i.e. the belief in universal rational standards, are mirror images of the same false epistemological stance. They are all underpinned by correspondence versions of our relations with reality. For relativists, there is no reality as such, so our thought cannot correspond with it. The perspectivist likewise downgrades reality, but would want to argue that different perspectives may offer complementary perspectives about life that do or do not conform more or less with reality. The rationalist position is also false because it posits a connection between reality and the judgements we make about it, and that in theory, though we might not always be right, we can know that reality. Thus Macintyre (1988: 358) can argue that:

> what is and was not harmless but highly misleading, was to conceive of a realm of facts independent of judgements or of any form of linguistic expression, so that judgements or statements could be paired off with facts, truth or falsity being the alleged relationship between such paired items.

Macintyre wants to suggest a different type of relationship between our judgements and reality. There are not two distinguishable items, judgements and that which is portrayed in judgements, between which a relationship of correspondence can hold or fail to hold. He wants to replace this correspondence theory with a different theory involving the relations between sets of meaning located within the tradition to which they belong. Traditions do develop and change, but not because they correspond more or less with a static and never-changing reality, but because contradictions and inconsistencies appear which demand resolution. They also change because they have to come to terms with ideas from rival traditions. There is always the possibility of epistemological crises, because rational inquiry is always dependent upon the relations within the particular tradition within which it exists. Knowing, therefore, always has to be located within particular ways of knowing, and is therefore always context-bound.

COMMUNICATIVE COMPETENCE

It is now worth looking at another attempt to resolve the dilemma identified above – that of developing a way of understanding the relation between text and reality which does not conflate the two. We have already made reference to Habermas's (1987) theory of 'the ideal speech community' (see Chapter 3), which is, as he suggests, an attempt to update and carry forward the Enlightenment project. For Habermas, statements about the world do not correspond to reality. Researchers cannot establish facts about the world; they can only, in seeking knowledge, reasonably argue. What does he mean by this? The truth can be established, and it may only be an ideal, if, in discourse, those elements that contribute to irrationality are excluded. This may seem to be tautological, but Habermas's twist on the dilemma allows a way out. If we can identify those elements that prevent us from reaching our ideal, we perhaps have a way of framing 'the pursuit of truth'. These elements would include relations of power between different protagonists.

Let us take an example: in a university, structured and differentiated as it is, with some people occupying positions of power and therefore, by virtue of their positioning, having a monopoly of resources, those with less power may feel constrained to express their views. So one principle would be that the consequences of arguing a case should not in any way be affected by other considerations. The communicative act is sealed off from the real world of differential positioning. However, we still have to confront a number of other problems and these comprise devices commonly used in language games. Rhetorical devices, such as concealment of position, irony, assertiveness, over-emphasis and the like, have to be removed from the equation because some are more skilled at their use than others. The language game must be played so that protagonists have equal resources, and this applies also to the level of information that each protagonist has to resolve the argument. Rapidly, we are cloning our two players in the game, so that they are bound to agree by virtue of being the same. But this involves a misunderstanding of the nature of the game, because all we are stripping away are those factors which comprise inequality and unfairness. Our two notional discussants coming from different positions, but without the impedimenta of differentiated positioning, may now debate and reach an agreement which is truly rational. Rationality is therefore inherent in properly conducted discourse or communication. There are two consequences of this approach. First, though Habermas is defending rationality, his defence is not that of equating it with reality. Rational agreement comprises consensus achieved when all the constraints to reaching such an agreement have been removed. Second, his approach is critical and emancipatory in that the 'ideal speech situation' is literally that, and impediments to it need to be examined and then dissolved. Furthermore, knowledge of those impediments (structural/ideological inequalities) goes some way to meeting these demands.

In Chapter 3 we suggested a number of problems with this position. However, what Habermas's 'ideal speech act' does do is point to the need to embed our ways of knowing within social and political arrangements. We therefore cannot simply dismiss power from our epistemological endeavours but must, as Habermas does, try to understand its effects. This involves a reflexive understanding of the way in which we are positioned as knowers, and it suggests that the scientific paradigm of a singular, convergent and fragmentable reality that can be known by researchers who act independently from the subjects of their research and who produce generalizations and nomothetic statements is not sustainable (cf. Guba and Lincoln, 1981). If, as many have argued, case study should be understood as paradigmatically different from traditional forms of research, then the argument for such a division rests on the ontological and epistemological factors discussed above. It also rests on those logical relations which underpin the construction of our research texts.

EIGHT

Observation

The next two chapters examine two different methods of collecting data. The first of these is observation. Observational techniques are much used in educational research, either on their own or to complement other strategies. There are a variety of approaches that researchers may adopt and these reflect their different purposes and different methodological frameworks. Gold's (1958) well-known typology of approaches range from participant observation to a complete observer role; they indicate particular understandings of the social reality under investigation and how researchers can know it. However, they also indicate particular research concerns and the issue of fitness for purpose will be one of the themes of this chapter.

PARTICIPATION

A number of dimensions structure the different approaches to the collection of observational data. The first of these dimensions concerns the role of the researcher. Participant observers argue that

> the social world is not objective but involves subjective meanings and experiences that are constructed by participants in social settings. Accordingly, it is the task of the social scientist to interpret the meanings and experiences of social actors, a task that can only be achieved through participation with the individuals involved. (Burgess, 1984: 78)

It is worth noting here that Burgess ties closely together data-collection and methodological framework. If the world is understood as consisting of individuals and collections of individuals interacting with each other and negotiating meanings in the course of their daily activities, then there is only one appropriate method, that of participation.

There are a number of possible reasons for choosing participatory methods.

The first of these is to secure access to the site under investigation. Unless researchers can offer something in return for being allowed entry to the setting, especially if it is a closed institution, they may be refused access. Here, participation is understood as a matter of establishing relations with participants in the research project, and its purpose is not directly related to epistemological and ontological assumptions about the act of research. However, the adoption of such an approach, even if this is not the intention, has implications for the type of strategy employed, the type of data collected and the type of conclusions that may eventually be drawn.

The second is to allow better access to the meanings of participants in the research, and this is because participants' meanings are frequently opaque, misleading and incomplete. A pre-determined observational schedule is too undiscriminating to allow the researcher to collect data about participants' interpretations of their actions. Furthermore, without some form of participation, there is no possibility of researchers understanding the effect that their presence has on the setting, which means that they are not able to construct reflexively the process of data collection they initiated. Those social markers – age, sex, ethnicity – which structure the type of interaction between researcher and researched remain unexplained and are therefore frequently ignored.

Participation may have a more profound purpose, which is that it allows researchers direct experience of the activities they are observing; thus, instead of understanding flowing from a detached stance, i.e. making a record of observations, participation now has direct experiential value. This means that the observer's account, though still a perspective on events that they did not initiate, has an added dimension: direct experience of the activities under investigation. This involves an act of imagination or identification which allows the observer 'to grasp the psychological state (i.e. motivation, belief, intention or the like) of an individual actor' (Schwandt, 1994: 120). Schutz (1967), however, suggests that this gives a misleading impression of how the researcher can understand social reality. For Schutz (1967: 159) it is much more a matter of grasping the intersubjective meanings given to their actions by social actors: 'the thought objects constructed by the social scientist, in order to grasp this social reality, have to be founded upon the thought objects constructed by the common-sense thinking of man, living their daily lives within their social world'. It therefore has little to do with experiencing the same type of activities and developing understandings by generalizing these empathized experiences, or intuitively getting inside that person's head. Consequently, there is bound to be a gap between the activities (intentions, beliefs, etc.) that precede actions and the observer's ability to grasp them.

If we accept this argument, then there may be a further reason for participating in the activities under investigation, and this is that in order effectively to understand the constructs used by participants, researchers need to understand both the context of the activities they were observing and how the data about them were collected. Researchers gain access to a site, for the purposes of collecting data, which they intend to leave having achieved their purpose. They are temporarily located in the site and this ephemerality means that they can never be full participants. They are always to some extent outsiders and this mindset is a part of their role as researchers. Schutz (1964), for instance, argues that researchers are never able to step outside themselves and live as natives. They are not able to bracket out completely their beliefs and epistemological frameworks through which they understand the world. They are, in effect, strangers who always retain vestiges of their original position and therefore can never quite go native. Translation, the key to understanding and then representing another way of life, is only possible from the standpoint of a set of values which are alien to the setting being studied. For Winch, this position is logically indefensible. The observer cannot stand outside but must participate. Only then can they write from the perspective which they wish to describe: 'Logical relations between propositions themselves depend on social relations between men' (Winch, 1958: 126). Archer (1988: 121) criticizes Winch for not being aware that there are universal rules which allow translation from one setting to another:

> Successful translation is a precondition of employing logical principles to attribute contradiction and consistency amongst alien beliefs or between those and our own. Unless we feel confident in the beliefs we ascribe cross-culturally, nothing can be said about these relations. This confidence rests on the conviction that it is possible to produce adequate translations of the alien beliefs.

The implication of this is that the observer, participating or not, may make use of constructs and concepts which are alien to participants in the social setting being studied. They therefore cannot, in a sense, participate fully, as they are involved in the act of translation and at the same time are making judgements (utilizing their value system) about the setting which they are investigating.

The other end of the dimension comprises a purely observational role in which observers seek to detach themselves from the social setting being investigated. Here, the intention is to behave as a fly on the wall and not disturb or change what is being studied. Except for the purposes of gaining access, the researcher interacts as little as possible with participants in the research. There are three reasons for this. First, this detached stance allows observers to gain a more comprehensive view of what is being observed – they are less likely to be influenced by the agendas of participants. Second, this stance allows observers to become more detached from their own specific agendas and from the way they are positioned (i.e. in terms of age, sex and ethnicity) in relation to the subjects of their research. Third, it allows them to gain a more objective view of the reality being investigated. As with any instrument, there are epistemological assumptions underlying its use. These assumptions comprise a belief that the preconceptions and viewpoints of the observers should not play a part in the particular construction of reality. Researchers are able to bracket out their own values and represent a reality which is not dependent on them as researchers. They merely act as conduits. Representation therefore becomes a relatively straightforward act (though various devices are set in place to check the reliability of the data collected, or to put it another way, to check that researcher bias does not enter into the research act). If, however, the research act is understood in Gadamerian terms, as a 'fusion of horizons' (Gadamer, 1975) in which the observer and the observed fuse their different versions of the world, then such a detached stance is considered illegitimate.

Gold's typology serves as an illustration of the extremes discussed above and of the various positions that researchers can take up in between. The key element of this particular dimension is that of participation (Figure 8.1).

Complete participant	Participant as observer	Observer as participant	Complete observer

Figure 8.1: Observational types

INSTRUMENT STRUCTURE

The second dimension is the structure of the instrument chosen to collect observational data. This has three elements – the first is the degree of control it allows the researcher to exert over the observational act. The second refers to when the focus of the observation is determined – whether, for example, it is pre-set, flexible or post-determined. The third concerns the type of closure involved in the analysis of the data. An example of an instrument which allows the researcher little control, because categories are pre-determined and the method of use is controlled, is the well-known system developed by Flanders (1970: 34):

1. *Teacher accepts student feeling.* Accepts and clarifies an attitude or the feeling tone of a pupil in a non-threatening manner. Feelings may be positive or negative. Predicting and recalling feelings are included.
2. *Teacher praises student.* Praises or encourages pupil action or behaviour. Jokes that release tension, but not at the expense of another individual; nodding head, or saying 'mm hm?' or 'Go on' are included.
3. *Teacher use of student ideas.* Clarifying, building or developing ideas suggested by a pupil. Teacher extensions of pupil ideas are included but as the teacher brings more of his ideas into play, switch to category 5.
4. *Teacher questions.* Asking a question about content or procedure, based on teacher ideas, with the intention that a pupil will answer.
5. *Teacher lectures.* Giving facts or opinions about content or procedures; expressing his own ideas, giving his own explanation, or citing an authority other than a pupil.
6. *Teacher gives directions.* Directions, commands or orders with which a pupil is expected to comply.

7. *Teacher criticises student*. Statements intended to change pupil behaviour from non-acceptable to acceptable pattern; bawling someone out; stating why the teacher is doing what he is doing; extreme self-reference.

8. *Student response*. Talk by pupils in response to teacher. Teacher initiates the contact or solicits pupil statement or structures the situation. Freedom to express own ideas limited.

9. *Student-initiated response*. Talk by pupils which they initiate. Expressing own ideas; initiating a new topic; freedom to develop opinions and a line of thought, like asking questions; going beyond the existing structure.

10. *Silence or confusion*. Pauses, short periods of silence and periods of confusion in which communication cannot be understood by the observer.

Other examples include systems developed by Galton *et al.* (1980) and Simon and Boyer (1970a, b, 1974). Pre-coded observation schedules yield data sets that are easier to analyse, because they are expressed in mathematical form and they can be effective instruments for gathering particular types of information, especially those with a tight focus and clear limitations. However, these systems, especially the more complex types, are difficult to administer. Furthermore, categories have to be devised that will cover all eventualities before observation takes place. Such instruments therefore require very careful preparation. Even with very sophisticated instruments, there are bound to be problems of interpretation, with events not quite fitting the pre-determined categories. They lack flexibility and cannot be responsive to unexpected events.

Pre-set coding schedules are usually based either on time or on an event. Event coding requires the identification of a particular event or events and the recording of them to allow a measure of frequency, both absolutely (number of occurrences) and relatively (frequency of different events). In addition, the design allows the observer to record the sequencing of such events. Events may refer to specifically delineated activities, i.e. types of talk, or to behaviours that are defined so that they are mutually exclusive and exhaustive (Robson, 1993). What this means is that a behaviour is defined so that it is not logically possible for another behaviour to be occurring at the same time (mutual exclusion) and that the total set of behaviours covers all the possible eventualities (exhaustiveness).

Control is most explicitly exercised through time coding of various types. The Flanders Interaction Analysis Categories (FIAC) referred to above constitute an example of interval coding. Instead of the occurrence of the event or the behaviour triggering a response by the observer, he or she will pre-determine an interval ratio, e.g. every minute, and then record the event or behaviour that is occurring. A more sophisticated variant of this is to have different types of coding for different time intervals. However, time controls make it more difficult for the observer to reconstruct the flow of events and sequences because of the gaps between observation periods.

Various devices to measure the reliability of such instruments have been developed. There are two main approaches: the first is intra-observer consistency, where the extent of concurrence between two observations (i.e. from a video-tape of a lesson in school) by the same researcher is measured; and the second is inter-observer agreement, where the extent of concurrence between two observations by different researchers is measured. Several statistical devices have been developed to enable the researcher to determine the degree of correlation between the different observations. However, it is important to recognize that these devices are measures of reliability and not of validity. Both sets of observations may be equally unrepresentative of the activities being examined. Finally, there is the possibility of observer drift – changes in the way in which the instrument is used over the period of the observation may cause a measure of unreliability. This may occur because of tiredness or over- or under-familiarity with the device.

These observational systems can be contrasted with the use of more flexible instruments, where the purpose of the observation is to be responsive to the nuances of social life and the meanings that actors ascribe to their activities. Observers acknowledge that they bring with them a set of constructs that structure their activity, so that they do not see the world anew, but in terms of previous knowledge of such settings. An example could be from Scott (1997b), during a project examining GCSE coursework completion in six secondary schools. Field notes record the following:

> I notice two girls sitting outside the headteacher's study reading books. At my last school pupils sent out of classrooms for misbehaviour were sometimes picked up by the Head and made to work for the rest of the day outside his study. I assume these two girls have fallen foul of some teacher.

Later, the observer is disabused of such a notion:

> The Deputy Head tells me that they try to welcome visitors by always having two girls on duty outside the Head's study, whose task it is to welcome visitors and ask them politely who they would like to see.

However, the intention is to build up a picture of what is being observed and understand it holistically.

The usual method of recording semi-structured observational data is by use of a record. Lofland and Lofland (1984) suggest five types of materials which might be included:

- Running descriptions – specific, concrete descriptions of events, activities and conversations
- Recalls of forgotten materials
- Interpretive ideas: preliminary analysis of the situation
- Personal impressions and feelings
- Reminders to look for additional information.

The advantage of these more flexible systems is that the researcher has not pre-judged the subject-matter, or at least is in a better position to correct observational errors. There is scope for the events themselves – what actually happens – to generate the analysis. Details about events and processes which might be omitted from pre-coded records or schedules are more likely to be included. The record generated by this method provides information about processes that is contextualized and may help to reveal connections and complexities that other systems preclude. On the other hand, with so much happening and no possibility of recording it all, this method can be difficult to use. In addition, the absence of a tight focus, which can be an asset of pre-coded systems, may make it difficult to decide what to record, and the unsystematic character of this method may make data difficult to analyse. Finally, the record is open to the charge of subjectivity – it cannot possibly be comprehensive, and little systematic attempt is made to eliminate researcher bias. The key element of this particular dimension is the control exerted by the observer in terms of their choice of instrument and how they use it (Figure 8.2).

Pre-coded time or event schedules	Observation schedules without systematic pre-coding	Flexible record

Figure 8.2: Observation schedule types

The three elements of this dimension may co-exist in different ways. Researchers may, for instance, focus on classroom talk and collect a full record of the exchanges between teacher and pupils during a particular lesson. Though a comprehensive record of the words used can be made – usually by audio or video recording – paralinguistic features such as facial expressions and eye movements may be more difficult to collect as data. Even if a video camera is used, it is generally assumed that it has to remain stationary so as to be unobtrusive, and is therefore likely to have been pre-focused on either the teacher, a child, a group of children or the whole class. These paralinguistic features provide the context for examining the meaning and significance of utterances and exchanges in educational settings. However, despite these difficulties, no attempt has been made, as with pre-set observational schedules, to predict or pre-determine the type of analysis that is subsequently conducted. This means that the data can then be construed in either quantitative or qualitative ways. Such decisions may be made after the collection of data.

FITNESS FOR PURPOSE

As we have stressed throughout this book, decisions about which methods to use depend as much on epistemological and ontological concerns as they do on the technical aspects of collecting data. This is disputed by Bryman (1988: 125), who argues that:

> The alternative position is to suggest that there ought to be a connection between epistemological positions and methods of data collection ... The problem with the 'ought' view is that it fails to recognise that a whole cluster of considerations are likely to impinge on decisions about data collection. In particular, the investigator's judgements regarding the technical viability of a method in relation to a particular problem will be important, as the technical version of the debate about the two research traditions implies.

However, it is difficult to see how these technical difficulties do not rapidly become epistemological and ontological difficulties upon closer examination. Some of the issues that have been examined in this chapter concern the practice of collecting observational data and may be expressed in terms of a series of questions:

- Should observers participate in the activities they are studying?
- What is the nature of that participation?
- What is the purpose of participation?
- Should the instrument used be pre-coded or post-coded?
- Should the instrument used be structured so that interpretations of events and activities take place before and after observation but not during fieldwork?
- Is it possible to develop a pre-coded schedule which takes into consideration the particularities and idiosyncrasies of student–teacher exchanges within classrooms?
- Which sites should the observer examine?

The answers to many of these questions will undoubtedly reflect the contingencies of collecting data and therefore be essentially a practical matter. However, lurking in the background are a series of issues that rightfully concern the epistemologist. For instance, the debate about participation is underpinned on both sides by a number of assumptions about the inquirer–subject relationship (whether it should be independent and detached or inter-related), about the nature of truth statements that emerge (whether it should be nomothetic or ideographic), and about the way observational data are inscribed in the research report (whether they represent in an unproblematic way what is happening or whether such surface data can capture the underlying reality which underpins them).

Furthermore, the debates expressed in this chapter about the structuring of the instrument also include viewpoints about whether we can or indeed should mathematically model social relations in classrooms, for example. For Bryman (1988), no necessary link has been established between epistemology and data-collection method. However, this lack of a necessary link is based on the observation that researchers who place themselves within interpretative or positivist–empiricist frameworks use similar methods or are prepared to use quantitative and qualitative techniques within the same research project. That they have not in the past addressed such issues or indeed taken account of them in the design of their research is no guide as to whether they should have. Fitness for purpose as a guideline has come to support a need to be methodologically eclectic. However, a more useful way of understanding it may be as a guide to whether relations between data-collection method, purpose *and* those epistemological relations which underpin method and purpose are in accord.

NINE

Interview Methods

Interviewing is an essential tool of the researcher in educational enquiry. This is because the preconceptions, perceptions and beliefs of social actors in educational settings form an inescapably important part of the backdrop of social interaction. However, there is a wide range of approaches, and these reflect methodological decisions about the rationale for using interview techniques. Interviewers differ about the degree of structure they should impose on the process, about its purpose, about its underlying rules, and about the epistemological assumptions which they make.

INTERVIEW STRUCTURE

A range of approaches from structured to life-history interviews is available. A survey researcher, for example, may seek to gather information about respondents' views on a number of different issues, but the method is pre-set; it involves the asking of precisely similar questions to large numbers of respondents who provide the interviewer with written answers. There are a number of implications. The first is that those issues which concern respondents are known in general terms before the questionnaire is constructed. The inflexibility of such an approach means that individual concerns, particular ways of understanding and personal life-history stories are ignored. Second, the purpose of using pre-set questionnaire methods is to gather information across a large number of cases, and therefore techniques for guaranteeing the reliability of the comparison between different sets of data from different respondents need to be set in place. To some degree, this emphasis on reliability is to enable the data that are collected to be expressed enumeratively. Third, the written dimension structures the type of data that can be collected, to the degree that it relies on, where the issues are about the meaning frames of respondents, the ability of those completing the questionnaire to express their thoughts in written form.

This is only one end of a spectrum, which ranges through structured interview techniques with pre-set and imposed schedules of questions to semi-structured approaches which allow the agenda to be constructed by the respondent. The structured interview may be understood as an alternative to the use of questionnaires, in that reliability of response between interviewees is still of paramount concern, but scope is provided for the elucidation of responses. This has the advantage that useful data can still be collected even if respondents have problems with expressing themselves in written form. Furthermore, this added flexibility allows interviewers the opportunity to frame and re-frame the questions so that they can be more certain that they are understood in the same way by all the respondents. In other words, by allowing the use of hints, prompts, and re-phrasing of questions, the interviewer can both ensure that respondents interpret the questions in the same way and be more certain that participants do in fact understand what they are being asked.

At the other extreme are semi-structured interviews in which respondents are encouraged to set the agenda of the interview, though the presence of an interviewer and other forms of control exerted by them means that the respondent never has full control of the setting. The interviewer sets up the interview, is involved in the negotiation of place, purpose and agenda at the initial stages, and, unless they remain silent throughout the interview, asks questions, prompts answers, and elicits reformulations of responses. Respondents provide answers and give accounts of their lives in terms of their understanding of the settings in which they are located. Thus gender, race, class and other types of power relations are conveyed by the researcher and form an essential backdrop to the answers that respondents provide. This can be illustrated by reference to adult–child interview settings. If the educational researcher is interviewing children within a school setting, each child will understand the role of the adult interviewing them in terms of the power relations in which they are located. In this case, they are more likely to respond as they would to their teacher and in terms of the codes they have been initiated into as a child/pupil/student. They read the signs and position their responses in terms of those signs. This does not mean that children *per se* should be understood in a homogeneous way, and the assumption cannot be made that they will respond in similar ways. The relationship between the giver and reader of those codes is never that simple. The setting in which the interview takes place is a depository of available meanings from which the interviewee draws in giving their answers. However, what a face-to-face encounter does do is to allow the interviewer to make a judgement about how those signs are being read and thus to locate their data in the contexts in which they were collected. A range of possible interview approaches may be displayed as in Figure 9.1.

Surveys and questionnaires	Structured interviews	Semi-structured interviews

Figure 9.1: Interview types

In a face-to-face encounter, the interviewer offers a number of clues as to how the interviewee should respond. This involves the content of each question or remark (the focus), the way in which it is asked or made (the frame) and the relations between the different questions or remarks (intertextual focus and frame). Focus may be defined as the extent to which the original agenda of the interviewer is adhered to; frame, on the other hand, is understood as the way in which that agenda is realized. In the first place, focus and frame refer to the linguistic features of the exchange. The frame, in part, comprises communicative devices such as irony, assertiveness, honesty and various ways of sustaining an argument, even if they are expressed as questions. However, the interviewer is also offering a number of paralinguistic clues to be solved by the respondent. These may comprise: type of dress, age and gender, voice intonation, the degree of turn-taking, the type of seating arrangements, the amount of physical intimacy between participants, and other features of the particular setting where the interview is being conducted. In the case of group interviews, there is a further dimension. These linguistic and paralinguistic features now refer to encounters between a number of individuals – their interactions both with each other and with the interviewer.

A research interview, unlike a conversation, also comprises a method for recording the information, though usually this only involves a record of the linguistic exchanges which took place. Whatever the method chosen, it is intrusive, and the degree of that intrusion contributes to its framing. If a tape recorder or video camera is used, this will affect the degree and type of privacy experienced by the interviewee, and may breach the public–private dimension of the exchange as it is understood by the person being interviewed. Again, this acts as a structuring device, as the use of a recording instrument signals that the data are public and therefore subject to the rules which structure public discourse. These are different from the rules which structure private discourse, and are well understood, even if tacitly, by participants in these research encounters. The interviewee may ask for the recording device to be switched off if they feel that what they want to say breaches the differentiating rule between public and private discourse which they adhere to. Other ways of recording data, i.e. making notes, are not so intrusive and therefore give off different messages to interviewees. However, because of the practical problems of making a full written record, the use of note-taking has the effect of introducing a formality otherwise not present. It therefore acts as a framing device; indeed, any method of recording data during an interview has this effect.

Other forms of control that can be exercised by the interviewer concern the promises made to the interviewee about the way in which their data will be treated. There are a number of possibilities: the integrity of the original data is preserved, with the interviewee not being allowed to change anything at a later stage; the interviewee is given the opportunity to change what they said by being offered the opportunity to edit either a transcript of the interview or the final report; or the research is so designed that it comprises a number of interviews with the same person, which means that the original data are superseded by later data and this gives the interviewee the opportunity to either make amendments or fundamentally change the direction and focus of their account. Each of these options implies a different epistemological position. In the first case, the data are treated as sacrosanct and reflective of an underlying reality. In the second case, an acknowledgement is made that the interviewee may be mistaken, and the opportunity is afforded to them to improve their account. Its underlying epistemology is still that of representational realism. The third case is more complicated. Here the interview is understood as dynamic and as constituting a continuous process of constructing and reconstructing past events or present opinions. It is the reconstruction itself which is the purpose of the exercise and not the gathering of data that represent in a straightforward fashion an underlying reality. Indeed, the interviewer acts as a change agent to enable the interviewee to readjust both their past and present understandings.

Perhaps the most important mechanism of control in an interview is its timing and how long it takes. This locus of control is determined by its closeness to the events or activities to which it refers. If the intention is to complement observational data, then its timing in relation to the original event will have an effect on the data that are collected. On the other hand, if the interview is specifically designed as autobiographical and refers to the life history of the participant, the timing of the interview is less important. However, since it is concerned with reconceptualizations of events in the past, recent events are likely to have more immediacy and to have undergone fewer reformulations. The timing of any interview is subject to the practicalities of setting it up in the first place. It may not be possible to arrange an interview at the most expedient time. Finally, the interviewer has to decide whether the agenda should be explicit or implicit; indeed, whether they offer a list of topics or questions to the interviewee before the event. If they do this, they are asking the interviewee to prepare their answers and an opportunity is being given for the presentation to reflect better how they would like their data to be treated in the final report. Some control over the agenda is being handed to the participant, or at least the reflective process which takes place during an interview is extended to a period before it.

The degree of structure within an interview is therefore determined as follows:

- the focus
- the linguistic and paralinguistic frame
- the data-recording method
- the agreed mechanism for data-collection and analysis
- the timing of the interview
- the explicitness of the agenda.

Following Bernstein's (1971) explication of the relationship between classification and framing, there is a similar relationship between focus and frame in terms of the relative strengths of each. A strong focus is understood as the exertion of a large degree of control by the interviewer over the contents of the exchange; correspondingly, a weak focus is defined as a limited degree of control exerted by the interviewer over its contents. A strong frame, on the other hand, would include items such as: tight control over the timing and duration of the interview, a blurring of the public–private dimension, no opportunities afforded to the interviewee for review or editing, the construction of a formal setting, and the use of a controlled linguistic/paralinguistic framework. A weak focus is defined in opposition to this. It is possible to locate different types of interview format (surveys/questionnaires, structured interviews and unstructured interviews) in relation to the two axes of Figure 9.2.

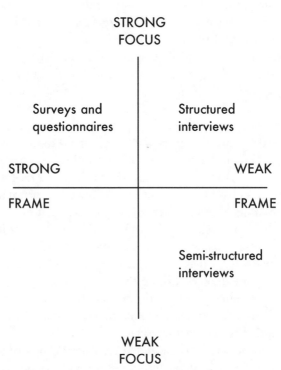

Figure 9.2: Interview focusing and framing

EPISTEMOLOGICAL AND ONTOLOGICAL FRAMEWORKS

Interviews may serve a range of purposes:

- They can allow access to past events.
- They can allow access to situations at which the researcher is not able to be present.
- They can allow access to situations where permission is refused for the researcher to be present.

- They may allow cross-checking against other data collected from different sources.
- They may be used to collect data about the belief systems and knowledgeability of individuals in society.
- They may be used to allow understanding of patterns within social life, where the emphasis is on the reliability of the data collected.

These different purposes connote different epistemological and ontological frameworks, and as a result interviewers who do not share the same perspective are likely to adopt different strategies. As we suggested above, this would mean that the interviews they conduct would be focused and framed in different ways. If the purpose is to collect attitudinal and informational data across a wide range of settings, then a strong focus and frame are likely to be preferred. If, on the other hand, the purpose is to collect data within particular contexts, or even to understand those contexts, the focus and frame are likely to be weaker.

This has implications for the epistemological and ontological frameworks within which interviewers operate. We have already made reference to four epistemological paradigms: positivism–empiricism, interpretivism, critical theory and postmodernism. Researchers from each of these will structure the interview in different ways and treat the data it provides differently. For example, positivists–empiricists seek to uncover patterns in social life by collecting facts (usually in quantitative form) about the world. The data-collection instrument, in this case the interview, plays no part in the determination of the truth-value of the data. Indeed, the instrument itself acts in a neutral capacity. However, the method still has to be standardized, to allow comparisons between different items of data. If, on the other hand, the researcher operates within a different framework, i.e. interpretivism, then the collection of interview data has a different rationale, and this is to allow access to the skilled performances of social actors. For Giddens (1984: 329), 'study of the structural properties of social systems cannot successfully be carried on, or its results interpreted, without reference to the knowledgeability of the relevant agents'.

This implies a particular ontological stance as well, in that agency and structure are now being treated as a duality. This has been disputed by, among others, Archer (1988), who argues that the relationship is better understood as a dualism. The debate is about the precise relationship between structure and agency or, in other words, whether structure is to be granted some freedom from what Bhaskar (1993: 154) has termed 'tendential voluntarism'. Can cultural properties, including systems of language, operate separately from, or at least not through, the skilled performances of particular individuals or groups. For Archer (1988: 89),

Nations can fall, polities be deposed and economies bankrupted, while efforts are being made to change the factors responsible (for example, birth rates, despotism, illiteracy, ethno-centrism). As a general theoretical proposition this holds good, however short the time interval involved. Yet this is what is spirited away by making all cultural properties atemporal and according them only a pale 'virtual existence'.

The precise relationship between agency and structure and how it is understood will determine the design of the research, the reasons for collecting interview data and the way in which they are collected (in other words, it will determine the interview's frame and focus).

POWER RELATIONS

The power relations which structure interview settings are never more obvious than when the biographies of the interviewer and interviewee(s) are inscribed in different social practices and discourses. Scott (1992) was employed by the *Voice* newspaper to research school experiences and career aspirations of Afro-Caribbean 16–30-year-olds. The research methods that were employed took two forms. First, a series of group interviews was organized with the intention of collecting qualitative data about the perceptions, aspirations and lifestyles of 'Afro-Caribbean' 16–30-year-olds. These group interviews took place in polytechnics, colleges of further education, youth clubs, advice centres, employment centres, health education centres, schools and community colleges. No attempt was made to organize representative samples of unemployed youths, students, users of youth clubs, etc. Second, a questionnaire was completed by 608 people. Three methods of contacting people were used. Those who took part in the group interviews were also asked to complete questionnaires. A small advertisement was placed in the columns of the *Voice* newspaper giving the name and address of the research organization and asking readers to send off for a questionnaire to complete. Finally, the questionnaire itself was reproduced twice in the pages of the newspaper, with a request to readers to complete it and return it to the researcher. Data-collection methods were therefore in the main postal, though a significant number of the questionnaires were completed in the presence of the researcher.

These are field notes (Scott, 1992) written directly after one particular fieldwork episode.

> This is an employment and youth training agency in the middle of a large city. I ring up and ask to meet a group of 16–30-year-old Afro-Caribbeans. I don't tell her that I am white, though if I had been asked to do so I would have done. My voice is middle class and educated; but that doesn't tell her anything, though she may have suspicions. I give my name. That's not conclusive either.
>
> I say that I represent the *Voice* newspaper. They all have, I presume, an image of this newspaper. It calls itself 'Britain's leading black newspaper'. It thus claims to represent the interests of black people in this country. When the organizer who works for the employment agency collected together a

group of people for me to talk to, I would guess that all she said was 'there is a researcher from the *Voice* newspaper who would like to talk to you about your experiences at school and at work'.

It takes place in the evening. I walk in, and though some people are clearly looking out for me, I am ignored temporarily. I don't fit the image of a researcher or reporter who works for the *Voice* newspaper. I introduce myself as the organizer emerges from a back room. We sit down and I say who I am and what my purpose is.

Though I have an agenda, it is quickly subsumed under theirs. Underpinning everything they say are two questions: am I on their side? how can I understand their fears, preoccupations and lifestyle? One participant wants to convince me that a black messiah is about to emerge who will lead 'black people out of the desert of white racism that they are presently in'. His imagery is biblical. I get him to talk about his school experiences. Everything is seen from the perspective of white racism: 'My teachers didn't like me because I'm black'; 'I didn't get in the football team because I'm black'; 'I was expelled because I'm black'.

I am being pushed into a corner. I am beginning to feel that I am responsible because I am white. I say how much I abhor racism. This is treated with a certain amount of contempt. Someone else starts to talk about immigration policies. Enoch Powell's Wolverhampton speech of twenty years ago is mentioned. I estimate that he was about five at the time. The same person then talks about Caribbean immigration. I ask him to be more specific, and I say (this is a mistake): 'Do you mean Jamaica?' I am immediately accused of stereotyping all immigrants as Jamaican, of simplifying a complex issue of nationality. 'That's typical', I am told, 'You all think we come from Jamaica'.

I then begin an extended dialogue with one of the participants about white racism, and how I must be racist because I am white. I defend myself and am then accused of being defensive, closed and determined to be separate. The only female participant (besides the organizer) says: 'Look at the way you are sitting, cross legged, arms folded. You are making yourself different'.

I get them back to talking about their experiences at school. One of them tells me about how black children are patronized and stereotyped. We move away from school life to the police. Someone tells me that he is on the run from them. Do I believe him? He tells me that he has in the past been taken down to the local police station and beaten up, and that they are looking for him. He tells me about the problems of being unemployed and in his case almost unemployable because he is black. He tells me that younger black people are ready to take to the streets again as they did in the eighties. Resentment and anger are bubbling up again.

And then finally, after about two hours, I am questioned about my research role. They say that I am not what they expected. They didn't expect a white university researcher. They expected a black reporter from the *Voice* newspaper. As I leave, someone says, 'Nice to meet you. But you'll never understand us. You've never been oppressed'. That's the bare bones of one particular research encounter in this project.

The members of this group were reacting to the persona of the white researcher as they understood it. These participant accounts were constructed by the occasion. The researcher was white, middle class, university educated, and well dressed. These social markers conveyed messages about power and authority and ownership of the data. We can speculate that they would have given different accounts of their experiences of education and work to a black female researcher with working-class roots. Knowledge of the biography of the researcher is therefore essential to understanding the type of data that are collected. Indeed, one can go further and suggest that the reconciliation of the different agendas in the final research report reflected the power relations of this and the other encounters. These relations were conveyed both by the way in which the interviews were focused and, more fundamentally, by the way in which they were framed. The spoken texts of the researched (constructed during the interview) and the written text of the researcher (constructed after the fieldwork had been completed) were therefore embedded within a set of social and political arrangements and could have been otherwise.

The form that a research report generally takes is realist and representative, thus conveying the impression that the researched account stands in some way for a set of phenomena that exist outside it and can be understood without reference to the way in which it was constructed. If this fiction is to be exposed, a reflexive understanding of the research experience is needed. This does not mean that the researcher simply has to supply a series of biographical facts to enable the reader to contextualize the account they are reading. The reflexive posture is more complicated. The researcher needs to understand that it is their sociality and the way that this is inscribed in social practices, language and discourses which constitute the research process (cf. Usher, 1993).

TEN

Biographical and Autobiographical Method

Erben (1996) provides us with a summary of the biographical method, and this discussion has resonances with many of the points made in Chapter 9 about interviewing. This is to be expected, since the autobiographical interview is central to an understanding of this approach. Erben summarizes it as follows:

- He quotes Denzin (1989b: 7) to the effect that the biographical method is 'the studied use and collection of life documents ... These documents will include autobiographies, biographies, diaries, letters, obituaries, life histories, life stories, personal experience stories, oral histories and personal histories'. Two types of texts are being referred to here: written records by and about individuals, and personal testaments recorded in the course of extended interviews. Though both are useful methods of collecting data, each has to be treated separately.
- Central to the ontology of the life-history method is the notion of 'narrative'. This refers to underlying patterns, usually in story form, that permeate individual experiences.
- There is a hermeneutic process at work in the collection of life-history material, which refers to both biographer and participant.
- The biographical method is an attempt to overcome the divide between structure and agency or to mediate between the structural and the phenomenological. It does this by focusing on the individual life, lived in terms of social narratives, institutional mores and those relatively enduring structures within which it is positioned. It therefore involves a reconciliation between dichotomies and between dichotomous methods.
- The central building block of the biographical method is the text, whether it be spoken or written, by the person or others. The method is also concerned with the biographical text that emerges from the process. Texts are situated in

history, and this historical dimension has implications for how they are constructed and understood.

- The life history focuses on the individual and is particularistic. It does this through narrative analysis, but always with the understanding that these narratives are public, even if made and remade at different points of time by the actions of individuals and groups of individuals.

- Central to narrative analysis is the notion of time. Time is understood as experienced through social narratives and provides a cohering character to that life.

- There are different versions of any life. Indeed, a definitive account of the life involves a misunderstanding of the nature of the method. This is so for two reasons: the life is immersed in history and therefore always realized within present ways of understanding, traditions of thought and inscriptive practices; and it is necessarily being constructed and reconstructed at different moments and in different ways by its author.

BIOGRAPHY/AUTOBIOGRAPHY

Two themes are central to this discussion of the method: the relation between biography and autobiography; and the relationship between the phenomenological and the structural. The biographer or educational researcher is engaged in a process of reconstructing the life from fragments of the data collected in the course of extended interviews. This involves a number of processes: gaining access to the material (choosing and negotiating with the person about the public presentation of their autobiographical text), collecting the data (either in the form of semi-structured interviews or through written documents), interpreting those data and constructing the account, reflexively surfacing their traces within it, and agreeing on the way it is to be inscribed.

Biographers come face to face with autobiographical texts situated in time and place. These are reconstructions by participants of their own fragmented lives. They are made coherent by an act of methodological introspection agreed between the participant and the researcher. These agreements are negotiated and renegotiated during the collection of the data and involve shifting power relations between the two participants as the account comes to fruition. However, what complicates the issue is the nature of that account, as it is delivered to the researcher.

The individual life is continuously made and remade by the participant in the present, to achieve narrative coherence. Since narratives are embedded in history, the life is always undergoing transformation. It is never enough to understand the process as one of remembering, or of course not remembering (given the frailty of memory), the past and then representing that account as truthful. Social actors literally reconstruct the past with reference to how they understand the present. Indeed, that understanding is a reconceptualization of previous reconceptualizations. The nearer in time the event or activity being recalled, the fewer re-representations there are. Indeed, the process is wave-like, as successive accounts are re-told and re-formed in relation to present understandings. It is further complicated by memory of overlapping reconstructions and by memory of how the event or activity was understood in the past. This meta-process of reflection has both a focus and a frame. It refers to the past, but it also refers to the way in which the past was, but is no longer, framed. Indeed, this understanding of the frame is reconceptualized by the social actor in the present.

The second element of the life is that it is fragmentary. This is not just because memory is fragile, but also because the original and subsequent reconstructions of events are particularistic. The social actor does not, and cannot, have full knowledge of the events and activities to which they refer in their autobiographical accounts. They cannot know (indeed, if they could, they would have a God's-eye view of what happened) the consequences of projects that they initiated. These are unforeseen. Furthermore, they may have a limited view of why they actually did what they did and of how they subsequently understood it. Tacitly, they may be 'skilled knowers' and may have a store of knowledge from which they draw in their everyday lives, but are unable to articulate it to themselves and in the course of a life-history interview. Indeed, those relatively enduring structures in which they are necessarily positioned as social beings are understood by them, whether tacitly or otherwise, idiomatically. They interpret them in ways that perhaps others would not. Though Bhaskar (1993) suggests that structures may have a real existence, the way they are known and therefore incorporated into the autobiographical account is determined by the research process itself.

This has implications for the biographer. The latter is complicit in the account, which always offers a different perspective on the life and indeed always goes beyond it. The researcher or biographer has their own biography, which comprises a set of presuppositions and is presently constituted. They are therefore positioned both biographically and in terms of those epistemological frameworks through which they know the world. The interpreted account is therefore only one of many interpretations which could be made; and furthermore it involves at some point a closure of the series of interpretations which are being made during the course of the research process. Though this implies that the biographer and the participant are unequally positioned in relation to this closure, this is to simplify a complex procedure. Biographers usually consult and negotiate about the completed account. Furthermore, they may be in sympathy with the project of the participant, and thus the closure they mediate is in accord with that of the participant. Indeed, if the life-history interview is to be understood as the reconstruction of a 'life', then a measure of agreement is generally reached. The account, as a result, conforms, to a greater or lesser extent, to particular agendas, and those agendas always make reference to the past of the biographer and to that of the participant. This is why commentators such as Erben (1996) frequently refer to the biographical method as autobiographical. The interpretive or hermeneutic procedure implicit in the biographical act is necessarily replicative of the process undertaken by the autobiographer.

PHENOMENOLOGICAL/STRUCTURAL APPROACHES

The second problem for the biographical researcher is the precise relationship between the agency of the individual and those 'relatively enduring' structures within which they are positioned. We have already suggested that the agency of the individual is in part constructed and reconstructed by the participant, both in the course of their life and by the biographical process. It is thus forever in a state of flux. Furthermore, we also suggested that those structural relations, including the way in which texts are produced, are in history and are therefore also subject to change. However, the most fundamental insight of the hermeneuticist is that these structural relations can only be known in the first instance through their reconstruction by the individual. The biographical interview is therefore central to an understanding of the way that the individual is positioned in relation to those relatively enduring structures which characterize human relations.

This debate was referred to in Chapter 9, and four possible positions were identified:

1. Structural influences may be understood without reference to the way in which they are conceptualized by individuals. Researchers therefore need to employ methods which accord with this ontological position.
2. The structures and mechanisms which underpin social life are competently reflected in actors' descriptions. In other words, social actors can give adequate accounts of their skilled performances under the right conditions, and these reflect how society works.
3. Agency and structure operate as a duality. Human beings are neither determined by external and influential forces nor free unconstrained agents, who operate without reference to those sets of relations and conjunctions which constitute society. Actors continually draw upon sets of 'rules and resources' which, once substantiated, allow social life to continue as they become routinized. Human beings make their world in the context of previous attempts by them and other people (this creates structural properties), and at the same time transform those structures and change those conditions which influence subsequent reconstructions of the world. Furthermore, while agency is responsible for structural transformation, it is also being simultaneously transformed itself. Structures therefore only have substance, and then only fleetingly in the skilled performances of actors within society. Data which refer to this are therefore essential elements in any biographical enterprise and their collection is a social and ethical affair (Giddens, 1984).
4. Giddens's 'tendential voluntarism' has been criticized by Archer (1988), among others, because it suggests too close a relationship between agency and

structure; indeed, that it is a duality. For Archer, social structures and systems always have a relative independence from the activities and beliefs of social agents. This sophisticated form of dualism therefore suggests a problem for the biographer. If structures are to be understood as relatively independent of the way in which particular individuals and sets of individuals live their lives (and subsequently understand their performances), then the biographical account is always incomplete. However, if the biographical account is understood as only one part of the mosaic of understanding, then its importance for educational researchers is assured. The recent interest by educationalists in the method attests to this.

THE USE OF THE LIFE-HISTORY METHOD

As Becker (1966) has argued, the collection of life-history data enables the researcher to build up a picture of the individual and the events and activities surrounding them, so that relations and patterns can be noted. Ethnographic and qualitative approaches have tended to concentrate on the present and have been criticized because they lack a historical dimension. The life-history approach enables the researcher 'to explore social processes over time and adds historical depth to subsequent analysis' (Hitchcock and Hughes, 1989: 186).

In particular, the life-history method has been used by educational researchers to develop understandings of:

- The process of change throughout a person's life: 'both in episodic encounters and in longer-lasting socialisation processes over the life-history' (Blumer, 1969).
- The group, whether professional, disciplinary or institutional (Ball and Goodson, 1985).
- The relational level and the different arrangements of relations between individuals, between groups and between individuals and groups over time (Goodson, 1985).
- The context of ideas about pedagogy which the individual teacher holds (Watson, 1976).
- Teacher biographies in professional self-development (Woods and Sykes, 1987).
- Pupils' experiences of transfer to senior school and the myths which surround the process (Measor and Woods, 1983).
- Relations between the life histories of teachers and the history of the school in which they work (Smith and Keith, 1971).
- How the problems of learning difficulties are experienced in schools (Dickinson, 1994).
- The adolescent lives of girls studying 'A'-levels (Mann, 1994).

Though the popularity of this method has declined in recent years with the marginalization of phenomenological approaches, it is still a potent and useful method for exploring educational issues.

THE TEXT

At the beginning of this chapter, we suggested that textual analysis is central to the biographical/autobiographical method. Indeed, we can go further than this and argue that all types of educational research have to concern themselves with textual analysis, not least in that the researcher will produce a text of their own. In Chapter 2, we discussed writing or the production of a research text. Here we concentrate on reading texts.

A number of approaches to reading texts, in particular historical texts, are possible:

- With the use of an intransitive historical method, the text gives up its meaning and this comprises an unequivocal interpretation. Meaning resides in the text itself and it can only be read in one way. This does not mean that it is always read in this way, since the reader still has to adopt the correct method – i.e. phenomenologically bracketing out their values (the reader is able to put to one side their preconceptions and prejudices during the reading), logically inferring meaning from text (the one correct way of deriving meaning from the assemblage of words and other paralinguistic forms is applied) and being comprehensive (the reading is not selective in any way). This correct reading does not necessarily equate with the intended meaning of the author, as the author may not themselves fully appreciate the meaning of the words that they are setting down on paper. Furthermore, the author may actually change their mind about what a text actually means. However, there is within the text being examined an unequivocal statement of meaning, which can only be captured by an ahistorical method.
- The text allows an unequivocal reading because that reading is consistent with the intentions of the author. Again, the reading comprises the use of a method which is ahistorical. As Dunne (1993: 108) puts it, 'Empathy was possible because in the end the adequate interpreter was "connatural" with his author and real historical understanding, paradoxically consisted in tearing away the veil of history so that this elemental connaturality could assert itself.' A number of implications follow from this. It is illegitimate to talk about a text being read in a number of different ways, since the author intended it to be read in one particular way. Since the purpose of reading a text is to reconstruct what was in the mind of the author and not to make sense of collections and arrangements of words, the text itself acts only as a piece of evidence, albeit an important piece, with which to reconstruct the intentions of the author. There are a number of problems with this. First, the author may not know their own authorial intention with the required degree of certainty. Second, the author may have deliberately created a 'writerly' text, so that their intention is to allow

multiple readings of the text (Barthes, 1975). The meaning does not, therefore, reside in the text itself, but in the way it is read. As Cherryholmes (1988: 12) argues: 'prior understandings, experiences, codes, beliefs and knowledge brought to a text necessarily condition and mediate what one makes of it'. Furthermore, the form of the text or the way in which the thought processes of the author are translated into textual form, i.e. its textuality, is in history, which complicates the process of inferring authorial intention from the text.

- The text and the way in which it is read are embedded in history. Heidegger (1962) points to the 'fore-structure' of interpretation, and he means by this that 'an interpretation is never a presuppositionless apprehending of something presented to us', but always involves a 'forehaving', 'foresight' and 'foreconception'. Historical texts are therefore read in terms of their pre-texts – each society has its own way of organizing language, discourses and writing, and thus any historical text has a form which is unfamiliar to the reader. Furthermore, each text has a subtext, that which operates beneath the text, but which gives it its meaning – those epistemologies and traditions of knowledge which are historical and which permit a particular reading (cf. Usher, 1997).

There are a number of solutions to the problems created by the argument that textual reading is immersed in history. The first is that any interpretation which is made is necessarily perspectival, and that is as far as anyone can go. The second possibility is that we can in some way transcend the historicality of our interpretative stance. Gadamer proposes this solution, though it is only partial. Instead of suggesting that an unequivocal reading of a text is possible, he does argue that if we can understand the different contexts and pre-texts of a text, then this in itself constitutes a superior way of reading it. For Gadamer, wrestling as he did with the respective claims of authority and tradition, reading a text can be a reasonable activity, provided we understand that he is not advocating an 'external' or 'objective' endorsement of authority. Reason is always subordinated to the claims of tradition, as he makes clear:

> That which has been sanctioned by tradition and custom has an authority that is nameless, and our finite historical being is marked by the fact that always the authority of what has been transmitted – and not only what is clearly grounded – has power over our attitudes and behaviour ... tradition has a justification that is outside the arguments of reason and in large measure determines our institutions and our attitudes. (Gadamer, 1975: 250)

Heidegger's insistence on the place of the 'fore-structure' in any interpretation we make is in large measure a reassertion of this position.

SUMMARY

The life-history text is constructed in the following way:

- Central to the text is the process of interpretation, and this comprises an interweaving of two agendas: those of the biographer and the participant. This 'fusion of horizons' (Gadamer, 1975) means that researchers are always immersed in perspectives and frameworks, and that the act of research is exploratory and developmental for both parties. The biographical text has to be understood in terms of the way in which it was constructed, and this includes the situated autobiography of the researcher.
- The past is organized in terms of the present; that is, present discourses, narratives and texts constitute the backdrop to any exploration of the past. It is not that a biography refers to actual events which are then imperfectly recollected, but rather that past events are interpretations undertaken by the person whose 'life' it is, and these interpretations always have a pre-text (Usher, 1997). Furthermore, this pre-text, comprising as it does the means by which meanings are organized in the present, always makes reference to other pre-texts in the past and supersedes them (Scott, 1998c).
- The public and private dimensions of the account are intertwined. Private acts are located in history and carried out in society.
- The 'life' is fragmentary, comprising parts as opposed to wholes, narratives that never quite come to fruition, disconnected traces, sudden endings and new beginnings.

PART THREE

Issues

ELEVEN

Ethics and Educational Research

We close the book with an examination of four issues central to researching education. The first of these is the relationship between epistemology and ethics. In Chapter 5 we suggested that experimental researchers understand ethical behaviour in a particular way. That is, they use strategies that implicitly suggest both a monolinear view of knowledge and a utilitarian view of ethics. Furthermore, their method is deliberately discriminatory because they offer control and experimental groups dissimilar treatments, even if they do not know until the experiment has been completed which of those treatments is of the greatest benefit. Their justification is that, even if one of the groups is discriminated against, the experiment provides knowledge of how society works, to the general benefit of all.

There are some important consequences of this approach. In the first place, a particular relationship between theory and practice is being invoked. Practical knowledge is designated as inferior to theoretical knowledge. The practitioner, because of the weight of evidence and because it is expressed in nomothetic terms, is obliged to follow precepts developed from it. We referred to this earlier as the technical-rationality model, and it implies a separation between theory and practice and a diminution of the latter.

The second implication of this approach is that, since knowledge is understood as nomothetic and therefore prescriptive, it would be unethical not to incorporate into practice those behaviours that it recommends. This ethical prescriptiveness is a logical consequence of adopting this epistemological position. We are therefore confronted by the familiar argument over ends and means. Deontological theories stress notions of duty, absolutism and the ascription of moral principles that apply regardless of whether those activities are understood as ends or means. These can be contrasted with utilitarian principles, in which means or the process by which ends are attained are always judged in relation to those ends. There are, of course, a number of problems with this, principally in how the practitioner or theorist defines the greater good or end. Is this to be understood as pleasure of the greatest number of people or some other designated benefit? Again, if means can be justified in relation to ends, does this sanction particular forms of human suffering if ultimately it leads to the greater good of the community? However, utilitarians of whatever sort argue that if there are certain good ends which have been so designated, then the fulfilment of those ends is merely a technical matter.

The third implication is a clear separation of epistemology and ethics. Knowledge production is understood as being outside the realm of ethics. The ethical dilemmas that researchers have to confront apply to the use of that knowledge and not to its production or construction. This assumes a particular relation between the knowledge producer or researcher and what they are researching: that the researcher's values, preconceptions and, indeed, interests are carefully controlled for during the act of collecting the data. The researcher is expected to behave as a neutral conduit. On the other hand, if the research act is understood in a different way, as the merging of different perspectives, the values of the researcher being central to the collection of the data and their analysis, then a different set of assumptions are being made about the relationship between ethics and epistemology. The implication of this is that the way in which a researcher behaves towards participants in their research determines the status of the data and any conclusions drawn from them. At the very least, this obligates the researcher to make explicit their behaviours, to allow the reader an opportunity to understand the researcher's role in the construction of the knowledge that forms the centrepiece of the report. Once again, if this argument can be sustained, a close relationship between the practical activity of the researcher and those epistemological and ontological relations which underpin educational research methods is being suggested. In other words, researchers who adopt different frameworks necessarily understand the ethical dilemmas of research in different ways.

If we understand data-collection as a social activity, the researcher in the field is confronted by a series of methodological dilemmas, partly ethical in character, the solutions to which determine the type of data that are collected. Those fieldwork dilemmas involve researchers in making decisions about how they should conduct themselves in the field and are therefore concerned with the rights and responsibilities of both researcher and researched. There are three possible models. The first – covert research – emphasizes the need to conceal from respondents the aims and purposes of the research and for the researcher to act in a clandestine way. The second – open democratic research – stresses the rights of participants to control which data are collected and which are included in the research report. The third – open autocratic research – argues the case against allowing respondents these rights of veto and therefore obligates the researcher to protect the interests of those who have agreed to take part in the research.

COVERT RESEARCH

The principle behind this strategy is that participants in the research will behave unnaturally if they are aware that they are part of a research project. The researcher may indicate their presence in a number of ways: by asking respondents to take various tests that they would not normally do (this may result in pre-test sensitization), by their presence as outsiders or strangers in settings in which they would not normally be present (e.g. classroom observations) or by deliberately setting up situations (such as interviews) that the participant would not normally understand as part of their everyday routine. The epistemological and ethical dilemmas are different in the three cases. However, all produce forms of reactivity, which, it is argued, falsify the data which are collected and conclusions drawn from them and therefore make it difficult to generalize from the case being investigated to other cases in time and place.

Covert researchers attempt to exclude or at least minimize reactivity by concealing their presence. This can be achieved in a number of ways. The researcher may simply not tell respondents who they are and what they are doing, and may adopt a role which acts to deceive participants into thinking that they have a right to be there. An example of this is provided by Hockey (1991), who, having had previous experience as a soldier, spent a considerable amount of time with a group of young squaddies, who assumed he was just another member of the group, on the streets of Belfast, in training camps and doing exercises in the Canadian wastelands. There are four issues involved. The first concerns his capacity to act as a participant, which he managed to carry off because of his previous experience. The second concerns the gaining of access, and this had to be achieved by seeking permission from the commanding officer of the battalion. So, though his 'subjects' were unaware of what he was doing, those in positions of power were. The third concerns his role as a participant: though acting as a soldier he had to make frequent excuses to record the data he was collecting, and, furthermore, he knew that his participation was only temporary. The final issue was that, for the sake of authenticity, he chose to deceive the squaddies whom he was researching. His argument was that they would not have accepted him as part of the group and therefore he would not have been able to conduct the research. This choice was even more stark for Fielding (1981), who spent time researching members of the National Front and who had to be even more circumspect, since breaking his cover could have led to personal injury.

However, there are forms of covert behaviour that do not necessarily involve complete deception of participants. One such is where the researcher dresses and behaves as the participants in the research. Phtiaka (1997), for instance, in researching deviant pupils in mainstream schools, employed certain forms of dress and behaved in certain ways that mimicked those of the pupils she was investigating. No attempt was made to deceive them about her purposes. However, she deliberately behaved in a way that she would not normally have done to effect a rapport with them. There is a sense in which all types of research involve minor deceptions or provide incomplete information when access is being negotiated. If the research design is emergent, so that choice of methods is dependent on the burgeoning theory, then the researcher is rarely in a position to provide a full account of their purposes to the relevant gatekeeper. Furthermore, as Hammersley and Atkinson (1983: 71) point out, it may not be prudent to give a full picture at the beginning of the research because 'unless one can build up a trusting relationship with them rapidly, they may refuse access in a way that they would not do later in the fieldwork'.

However, the issue is not primarily about deception, but about validity. In some situations, such as those encountered by Hockey and Fielding, being open and honest would have fundamentally changed the situation. The 'squaddies' would not have behaved in a natural way and may have sought to offer a skilled presentation of their lives. Again, with members of the National Front, Fielding would have been unable to complete the research because he would have been seen to break their codes of secrecy. In some situations the presence of the researcher is marginal to the activities being examined, e.g. in a classroom setting where pupils are either familiarized to such practices or not sufficiently aware of them, so that it does not affect their behaviour. In other situations, such as in semi-structured interviews, the intention of the researcher is to participate in the construction of an account of the life and activities of the person being interviewed. Reactivity, rather than being understood as a negative consequence of research and something to be eliminated if at all possible, is embraced. A close relationship between data, method and theory is therefore accepted and thus the data are as much a product of the method chosen as being descriptive of any underlying reality.

OPEN DEMOCRATIC RESEARCH

Simons (1988) has suggested that open democratic procedures should adhere to five principles. The first is that the researcher should act impartially, i.e. 'withhold their judgements' or bracket out their value positions to allow an unbiased collection of views to emerge. It may be that these views represent a range of contradictory opinions. However, the democratic evaluator/researcher is enjoined to suspend the interpretative procedures they would normally go through. The second principle is to allow participants in the research a right of veto over the release of their data, and this should be exercised at every stage of the proceedings: the right to read and amend interview transcripts; the right to change, either by excluding or including, information in the report; and the right to control the release of the data either in their raw or organized form. The third principle is that this right should be exercised in the form of negotiations between researcher and researched, and every effort should be made by the researcher to provide enough information about its release into the public arena for the negotiation to be fair and informed. The fourth principle is that researchers should not in any way compel participants to take part in the research, and this may involve resisting imperatives from powerful people in the organization. Finally, there is the question of accountability. Democratic researchers argue that they are accountable not just to participants in their project but also to other bodies in the public arena with an interest in the information collected.

A number of questions need to be asked about this approach:

- Can the evaluator remain impartial and withhold their judgement in description?
- What does it mean to report 'accurately and fairly whatever transpires'?
- Should all participants have equal access to the data once they have been negotiated?
- Should respondents have a right of veto over use of their data or any other relevant data that have been collected?
- Should respondents have the right to 'correct or improve' their statements?
- Should the identities of participants in the research be concealed?
- Do respondents have the expertise to decide whether information about them should be placed in the public domain?
- Should the boundaries of the study be negotiated between the researcher and all the participants?
- Should release of reports/statements be negotiated between the researcher and the participants?
- Is it realistic to argue that criteria for negotiation of release of data can be fairness, accuracy and relevancy?
- Do participants have adequate knowledge of data-collection, data analysis, report-writing and, more crucially, dissemination to enter into proper and equal negotiations for release?
- Is the researcher in a position to ensure that every participant in the research project is not subject to coercion or pressure and is able freely to decide about their participation?
- Given the timescale and available resources of most research projects or evaluations, is it realistic to accept that every level and stage of proceedings should be subject to review by all the people concerned?

Democratic researchers accept that they bring to the setting a variety of prior ideas about the world, but assume that they can bracket out this knowledge and thus construct reality without reference to their own beliefs and pre-judgements. They are thus committed to present as full a picture as possible of what is going on by referencing social actors' perceptions of reality. This is in essence the phenomenological approach. Researchers deliberately write themselves out of the picture, and more importantly they do everything in their power to present a full account, through participants' words, of that reality. In effect, they deliberately diminish or conceal the reflexive element implicit in the process. This has implications for the power relationship between researcher and researched. They are denying, though this is of course theoretical and not real, their right to interpret the data they receive. They are therefore to some extent handing control of those data to participants in their research. They are allowing those participants a veto over how their lives and activities are inscribed in the report.

On the surface, this seems relatively straightforward. However, there are two major problems. First, each participant constructs their own account in terms of their knowledge of the circumstances in which that account is produced. Those circumstances might include how the participants understand what is expected of them and how that account will be received when it is inscribed in the text. It might be a deliberate response to the persona of the researcher – much feminist research works on the assumption that only a woman, with her inbuilt sympathy, can gather authentic data about other women (cf. Reinharz, 1992). Accounts, therefore, are always, in effect, presentations. Second, this phenomenological perspective assumes unjustifiably that participants have full knowledge of the perspectives that underpin their everyday actions. In other words, social actors are not able to transcend the limitations of consciousness. This can be expressed in four ways: human beings do not have full knowledge of the settings which structure their activities; human beings cannot have knowledge of the unintended consequences of their actions, because the translation of intention to fulfilment of project is never unproblematic, and furthermore, what actually happens is the consequence of the sum of a multitude of human projects which have unforeseen consequences; social actors may not be aware of unconscious forces that drive them towards projects which, consciously, they do not wish to complete; and social actors operate with tacit knowledge that they are either unable to articulate or unaware of as they go about their lives (cf. Bhaskar, 1989).

However, the principal flaw is that, to borrow Habermas's (1987) concept of the 'ideal speech situation', which is essentially a fictive notion, research data cannot be collected in ideal circumstances. This is not to deny the potential rationality inherent in good research, but to suggest that in real life only a limited form of rationality can exist. This is because those factors which mitigate against the ideal of a free, open and uncoerced exchange of views are ever present in evaluation and research settings, constructed as they are in terms of vested interests, inadequate exchanges of information and differential amounts of power between participants, be they sponsors, managers, participants or other stakeholders. As Norris (1992: 134) suggests, the ideal speech situation is

> a regulative idea (in the Kantian sense) which manifestly cannot be realised under present conditions, but which holds out the prospect of a genuine dialogue – an uncoerced exchange of differing arguments and viewpoints – from which truth might yet emerge at the end of the enquiry.

In addition, the deliberate bracketing out of the values of the researcher so that they operate from a set of values that is universal in orientation (no researcher can, of course, operate in an ethical vacuum) and that represents something which transcends the limited and everyday perspective of the researcher (in effect, a God's-eye view of reality) is not a practical possibility. This position, of course, does not rule out the possibility of adopting a reflexive posture in which those relevant values which drive the research at every moment and at every stage are identified and inscribed in some form or other in the report. Likewise, negotiated control mechanisms and, indeed, negotiated processes of deciding which data are to be collected, how they are to be collected and how they are to be inscribed cannot be achieved, but serves, in Norris' words, as 'a regulative ideal'. The researcher, in short, always understands the consequences of the release of data into the public domain better than participants in the research, though of course their understanding may be incomplete.

Democratic researchers propose a highly idealized form of research, in which two main purposes sit uneasily alongside each other. In the first place, they stress forms of external accountability which include the right to know by various public bodies, and in the second place, they acknowledge that research settings (these are understood in their widest sense and incorporate a variety of stakeholders) are hierarchically arranged and thus the publication of members' accounts is potentially dangerous. The implication of this is that the researcher may have to filter out knowledge which could potentially harm participants, even if those dangers are not apparent to the participants themselves. Regardless of the forms of negotiation undertaken by the researcher and those being researched, an ideal speech situation cannot exist and thus ultimate responsibility for the release of information must stay with the researcher/evaluator. This is because social actors in time and space have different and conflicting levels of knowledge about the setting. In short, in order for evaluators and researchers to proceed, they have to take account of the power structures in which they are working, and this involves the adoption of other approaches.

OPEN AUTOCRATIC RESEARCH

If research is to be understood as a deliberate closure by the researcher of interpretative procedures, whether they be further interpretations by the researcher of their previous interpretations or negotiations between participants and researchers about what is an acceptable account when it is placed in the public domain, then this has certain implications. The first has already been alluded to, and this is that the rationale for that closure, and indeed the form it will take, has to be made explicit, in so far as this is possible, to the reader of the report.

The second implication is that the researcher has to make a series of judgements about how that report will be received in the public sphere, and that this may involve deception when he or she feels that protecting the interests of participants in the research warrants this. Indeed, as Burgess (1984:197) argues,

fieldworkers are constantly engaged in taking decisions about ethical issues in both 'open' and 'closed' research; they are involved in arriving at some form of compromise, whereby the impossibility of seeking informed consent from everyone, of telling the truth all the time and of protecting everyone's interests is acknowledged.

The third implication is directly epistemological in character. This is that the researcher needs to accept that the ethical decisions they make regarding such issues as being sensitive to the needs of participants, even if those needs are not fully recognized by those participants, assuring anonymity to them so that they cannot be identified by other people within or outside the setting, since this has the potential to do them harm, and creating a consensual relationship with participants which means that those participants are not compelled to provide them with data, are in fact also epistemological decisions or at least have epistemological consequences. The argument revolves around the issue of interpretation, how those interpretations are made, and at what stage or for what reason the interpretative procedures are brought to a close. Inextricably linked, therefore, with the act of producing knowledge are issues to do with the rights, responsibilities and activities of participants in the research. Since these are affected by fieldwork decisions made by the researcher, who is always engaged in ethical activity, ethics and epistemology cannot be conveniently separated.

TWELVE

Evaluation and Research

One of the enduring controversies in educational research is the distinction drawn between evaluation and research. This is further complicated by their embeddedness within separate disciplinary matrices, each having different criteria for use, different methodological procedures and different ways of disseminating findings. Glass and Worthen (1971), for example, cite 11 factors which distinguish evaluation from research:

- *The rationale for the enquiry* – research is understood as the production of knowledge pursued for disinterested reasons, whereas evaluation is understood as a practical activity designed to provide solutions to real-life problems.
- *The aims of the enquiry* – research is understood as the collection of authoritative data and the drawing of definitive conclusions, whereas evaluation is designed to contribute to better decision-making in practical situations.
- *Laws as opposed to descriptions* – research is nomothetic in orientation and therefore attempts to establish law-like propositions about human relations, whereas evaluation is ideographic in form and focuses on particular cases or events.
- *The nature of explanation* – research is ultimately concerned with why or how questions, such as whether and in what way race impacts on social relations within schools; evaluation is concerned with effectiveness, above all with the success or otherwise of particular programmes or interventions.
- *Autonomy and control in the enquiry* – researchers are able to set their own boundaries for the enquiry, whereas evaluators always have to take into consideration the wishes and desires of the various stakeholders, in particular funders, with regard to the shape of the evaluation and the direction in which it should go.
- *Relation to social utility* – research is designed to provide authoritative knowledge about social processes which indirectly informs policy-making;

evaluation is concerned to provide prescriptive knowledge which directly influences policy-making processes.

- *Scale of the enquiry* – research is concerned with larger issues of social importance; evaluation concentrates on smaller and more carefully delineated processes and procedures.
- *Interpenetration of values* – research offers value-free knowledge of social processes in which the preconceptions of the researcher are methodologically bracketed out and do not 'contaminate' or affect the data which are gathered; evaluation is value-impregnated and has to concern itself with the values both of the evaluator and of those being evaluated.
- *Methods of enquiry* – researchers who seek generalizable knowledge employ methods which are appropriate to experimental and correlational designs, whereas evaluators generally use methods appropriate to ethnographic and case study designs.
- *Criteria for making judgements* – good research is defined in terms of its ability to meet criteria such as sound internal validity, credible external validity, reliability and objectivity; evaluation is judged by other types of criteria that emphasize action perspectives and the making of practical judgements. Guba and Lincoln (1985), for example, argue that evaluators should concern themselves with the evaluation's credibility, transferability, dependability and confirmability.
- *Disciplinary focus* – researchers operate from one clearly defined disciplinary perspective, whereas evaluators draw inspiration from a number of different perspectives.

Before embarking on a discussion of the various issues raised by Glass and Worthen (1971), it is worth examining the underlying epistemological and ontological assumptions of the distinction they make. Denzin (1989) suggests that the positivist–empiricist paradigm can be encapsulated in the following way: objective reality can be grasped, and researchers can remain neutral and bracket out their values from the process of enquiry; observations and generalizations are atemporal and asituational; and enquiry is considered to be an objective activity. Research, for Glass and Worthen, is therefore judged by four criteria: representational value, applicability, consistency and neutrality. They argue that it is an 'activity aimed at obtaining generalizable knowledge by contriving and testing claims about the relationships amongst variables or describing generalizable phenomena' (Glass and Worthen, 1971: 153). This is a model of research taken from a natural science perspective. Evaluation, for them, is understood in opposition to this and as embracing interpretivist perspectives. They therefore conclude that these latter perspectives do not constitute the proper business of research and are therefore inferior.

Smith (1982) provides a model of the relationship which draws the two closer together, though he still wants to understand them as separate activities. Indeed, by setting them in opposition to each other, though blurring the boundaries, he is suggesting that there is a meaningful distinction. Smith argues that evaluators: may be more concerned to assess the achievement of desirable goals; may be more constrained by the needs of stakeholders with their own vested interests; may have less control over choice of research methods and methodology; may be more circumscribed by time constraints; and may generally seek to influence decision-makers rather than provide generalizable knowledge about educational activities.

These distinctions involve both practical and methodological dilemmas that centre around the indubitably stratified nature of the settings that evaluators and researchers work within. There are three sites of data formation: relations between the researcher/evaluator and participants in the research; relations between participants and the settings in which they work, these settings being defined both allocatively (the stratified arrangement of material features of the environment and the means of material production and reproduction) and authoritatively (the structured organization of time–space, the body and life-chances in society) (Giddens, 1984); and relations between the researcher/evaluator and the external world. The last of these comprises the cluster of peoples who have a direct interest in the results of the evaluation, i.e. programme makers, funders, etc. and indirectly the general public. It should be noted here that both research and evaluation are embedded in these stratified settings, because, regardless of the paradigmatic perspective adopted, data-collection cannot avoid issues of power.

In Chapter 11 a fuller discussion of one evaluative model that attempts to provide a solution to the dilemma of meeting the different needs of stakeholders was presented. Briefly, democratic evaluators (cf. Simons, 1984) suggest that control of the data-collection process should comprise negotiated agreement between the researcher and those they are researching. There are three problems with this stance. First, negotiations are likely to take place between partners with unequal amounts of knowledge and resources. The researcher/evaluator is in a better position to understand the complex network of power relations which comprise the setting. Second, participants in any research/evaluation may not be in a position to understand fully their own role in the activities being evaluated. Third, the values of the researcher/evaluator form an essential backdrop to the design of the research/evaluation, to the fieldwork process and to the writing of the report that is subsequently produced. If social life is conceptualized as a dynamic and ever-changing phenomenon, then both evaluators and researchers have to operate within these constraints; that is, both the ontological and epistemological relations which underpin their work will structure it in a certain way.

However, the most fundamental difference between the two is in terms of what is being evaluated or researched. Evaluators are more concerned with assessing the effectiveness, or describing the impact, of a deliberately engineered social intervention. This social intervention may be initiated by a group of people who are external to the setting, i.e. policy-makers or curriculum designers, or internal to the setting, i.e. teachers in a school. Furthermore, these same initiators may then take on a different role with regard to the evaluation, i.e. in the case of policy-makers as commissioners of evaluation, or in the case of teachers as participants in the evaluation exercise, whether conducted by themselves or some external consultant. Those different stakeholders may therefore have a vested interest in the evaluator drawing certain types of conclusions about the effects of an intervention and moreover seek to influence the conclusions the evaluator comes to. Researchers do not operate with such a close relationship between themselves and the initiators of those interventions, though they still may be dealing with the effects of policy interventions, since these are an abiding feature of educational systems. These points may become more apparent if a particular evaluation is described (Scott *et al.*, 1997).

THE EVALUATION OF THE NATIONAL LITERACY ASSOCIATION (NLA) DOCKLANDS LEARNING ACCELERATION PROJECT

The evaluation team was contracted to collect data about the activities and effects of the Project as it was being implemented in 15 primary schools in the London Docklands area. The evaluation was designed to:

- measure the increase in literacy skills of about 500 pupils over a two-year period;
- aggregate these data at group and school levels;
- make a judgement of the value added by the school and/or group;
- identify and examine the various processes by which learning acceleration is hoped to be achieved in the classroom;
- examine childrens' attitudes towards reading, books, writing, classroom participation, thinking, solving problems, decision-making and applying learning in other contexts;
- collect data about school attendance and exclusions for the cohort of children during the two years of the project;
- identify and examine these various processes as they relate to the home, the family and the community.

As a result of collecting these data, it was envisaged that the evaluation would allow judgements to be made about:

- the most effective contexts and conditions for improving literacy, in particular with low-achieving pupils;
- structural, systemic and organizational barriers to the development of literacy in inner city schools;
- the effectiveness and efficacy of the Learning Acceleration Project in terms of the following aspirations:

  1. to achieve at least a doubling of the present rates of acquiring literacy skills in English in participating schools and to ensure that low-achieving pupils benefit just as much as their peers (e.g. pupils leave Docklands Primary Schools reading at a level appropriate to age and ability).

2. To enable teachers in participating schools to make constructive use of English and maths software including Integrated Learning Systems, in helping to develop childrens' basic skills, learning and problem solving.
3. To increase motivation, time on task and cooperative classroom behaviour in participating classes and improve school attendance rates where appropriate.
4. To foster parental/community involvement in support of literacy and related IT-based communication skills. (Project Document)

The National Literacy Association Docklands Learning Acceleration Project was funded by the London Docklands Development Corporation and managed by the National Literacy Association. It was a two-year project (1995–97) aimed at improving literacy and other basic skills among a cohort of year 3 (1995–96)/year 4 (1996–97) children in 15 schools in three London Boroughs (Southwark, Tower Hamlets and Newham). Its principal method for achieving its aim was through the implementation of an Integrated Learning System. This multi-media computer-based programme of structured learning and assessment (Global Learning System) was introduced into the schools in 1995. In addition, all the schools were issued with Acorn pocketbooks. The four Newham schools were not given the hardware supplied to the other schools but only the Acorn pocketbooks. They were already using 'traditional software for dedicated machines' acquired from previous projects (Table 12.1).

Table 12.1: IT hardware and software in the 15 schools

Southwark:

School 1	10 machines, 30 Acorn pocketbooks, Global Learning System
School 2	10 machines, 30 Acorn pocketbooks, Global Learning System
School 3	10 machines, 30 Acorn pocketbooks, Global Learning System

Tower Hamlets:

School 4	10 machines, 30 Acorn pocketbooks, Global Learning System
School 5	10 machines, 30 Acorn pocketbooks, Global Learning System
School 6	10 machines, 30 Acorn pocketbooks, Global Learning System
School 7	10 machines, 30 Acorn pocketbooks, Global Learning System
School 8	10 machines, 30 Acorn pocketbooks, Global Learning System
School 9	10 machines, 30 Acorn pocketbooks, Global Learning System
School 10	10 machines, 30 Acorn pocketbooks, Global Learning System
School 11	Acorn pocketbooks

Newham:

School 12	30 Acorn pocketbooks
School 13	30 Acorn pocketbooks
School 14	30 Acorn pocketbooks
School 15	30 Acorn pocketbooks

The project team organized INSET for the schools during the first year of the project (examples are provided in Table 12.2), and upgraded that training during the second year. In the first year, INSET was designed to meet the general needs of all the project teachers in the 15 schools.

Table 12.2: INSET for the schools provided by the Project 1995–96

May 1995	Initial training in ILS	8 schools	1 day
June 1995	Initial training in pocketbooks	5 schools	1 day
September 1995	Children recording their own progress	11 schools	1 evening
October 1995	Using 'Widget' in the classroom	5 schools	1 evening
November 1995	Making resources	4 schools	1 evening
January 1996	Initial pocketbook training	6 schools	1 afternoon
February 1996	Poetry workshop	7 schools	1 evening
February 1996	Follow-up pocketbook training	7 schools	1 afternoon
February 1996	Sharing pocketbook training	5 schools	1 evening
May 1996	Library links	4 schools	1 evening
May 1996	Reporting and monitoring	6 schools	1 evening
June 1996	'How can it help?'	3 schools	1 evening

At the beginning of the second year, the project team met with headteachers and planned specific INSET to meet the continuing needs of their schools in the second year. They also initiated a range of other activities; examples are provided below:

- Attending parents' evenings to raise the profile of the project.
- Organizing Parental Accreditation Courses for the pocketbooks.
- Introducing new types of software and hardware into the schools, such as: Textease, more pocketbooks in the Newham schools, batteries and battery chargers, printers, and new compact disk software.
- Organizing surgeries in the three boroughs.
- Arranging INSET about ILS recording and monitoring, and parental participation with the pocketbooks.
- Resolving hardware and software technical problems.
- Liaising with OFSTED inspectors.
- Establishing links with: local authority libraries, the TOWER Project for children with severe disabilities, the British Dyslexia Association, and the Open School for excluded children.
- Introducing poetry sessions in local libraries; liaising with local education authorities; working with the National Literacy Centres on classroom materials; advising on literacy testing for SCAA; providing consultancy in different parts of the country; and developing materials for Global English, Part 2.

Global English and the pocketbooks

Global English Part I concentrates on phonological and word recognition skills and consists of four modules: Words, Sentences, Spelling and Rhymes. It is complemented by a number of Active Books which digitize 'speech at the word, phrase and sentence level', and in addition offer 'different speeds of presentation, a context-sensitive talking dictionary, a built-in bookmark with summaries of "the story so far", an accumulating concept map and challenging comprehension tasks' (Moseley, 1995). Global English, as a whole, has been designed to have:

- an emphasis on units of meaning at all levels from letters to complete passages
- highlighting of words, phrases and sentences accompanied by high quality speech
- fluency building by advanced speed-reading techniques
- a structured multi-sensory approach to phonics teaching, complementing a 'whole language' approach
- no artificial restrictions in terms of vocabulary and phonics
- a talking dictionary which gives the meaning of words and phrases without leaving the page
- systematic means of teaching new concepts and extending vocabulary
- extensive use of propositionally-structured concept maps
- a 'Parrot Mode' facility for improving expression and clarity of speech
- ways of enabling pupils with learning difficulties to access meaning and strengthen areas of weakness
- cross-curricular relevance, with a problem solving emphasis
- a choice of voices for spoken help, support and reward
- a monitoring system for individual and paired reading (Moseley, 1995).

In addition, there is a Global Mathematics Programme. This Global Learning System was evaluated during its development in a small number of schools. The results were inconclusive due to an incompatibility between the hardware and software. However, Underwood *et al.* (1995) noted that no significant differences were recorded at key stages one and two in literacy or numeracy progress between the experimental and control groups. The Acorn pocketbooks include a wide range of programmes: a word processor (with spellchecker, thesaurus and dictionary), a data-handling package, 'Cards' (originally intended for keeping names and addresses), 'World' (this gives the time in any part of the world), a diary, a calculator, an alarm and a facility for voice recording.

Phase one of the evaluation

The first phase of the evaluation comprised the collection of quantitative data about literacy development in the 15 schools. In these schools, all the children who were in year 2 during the school year 1994–95 were assessed on a range of vocabulary, reading and spelling tests towards the end of the summer term 1995, or, in the case of two schools, at the beginning of the autumn term 1995. During the following two years, 1995–97, all these children received a range of interventions (see above) to improve literacy. The interventions varied from school to school, with some having a greater impact than others. At the end of the summer term 1996 and, in the case of two schools, at the beginning of the autumn term 1996, the children were reassessed, along with any children who had joined the school during that year and children who had been absent at the first assessment. The children were further tested during the summer term 1997, at the end of the project. Data were also collected from the schools about sex, age, free school meals, ethnicity and English as a first language at the level of the individual pupil.

Phase two of the evaluation

Phase Two of the project took place between September 1996 and July 1997. It comprised the following.

- Sampling six of the original fifteen schools for more intensive study and comparison. This sampling drew on the results of the school rankings in terms of childrens' progress in reading and spelling. It was also informed by information collected from the project team regarding the nature of the programmes in the different schools.
- Collecting observation and interview data from nine schools in November and December 1996 (half-day visits).
- Collecting observation and interview data from the other schools between January and April 1997 (three-day visits).
- Interviews with teachers. These focused on: changes that teachers have implemented in their classrooms as a result of the Project; strategies they have developed for low-achieving pupils; strategies for book use and reading; systems for enabling children to write with confidence and fluency; pedagogic and organizational strategies within the school and in the classroom to enable pupils to ask appropriate questions, acquire new concepts and vocabulary, think creatively, solve problems, become more effective decision-makers and be in a position to apply their learning in other situations; ways in which they use computer software and how this is integrated into their overall pedagogic strategies; pastoral approaches, in particular as these impact on classroom behaviour, school attendance and exclusions; and systems for involving parents in the teaching and learning processes essential to the development of the skills referred to above.
- Interviews with the children. These focused on: the demands made on them in school and at home, and in particular the demands made on them as a result of the Project.
- Interviews with parents. These focused on: relations between home and school;

the demands made on their children by the school; the impact of the Project; and their desires and wishes in relation to the educational experiences of their children.

- Collecting attendance and exclusion data (between January and April 1997).
- Testing the children in the smaller sample in writing between January and April 1997.
- Re-testing the children in July 1997 (reading and spelling).

The design of the evaluation was quasi-experimental. The programmes were made available to children and teachers in 15 schools in the Docklands area of London. The cohort of children was tested (using standardized reading, spelling and writing tests) at three points of time: before the intervention, half-way through and at the end. No comparison groups were used and it was accepted that the groups in the 15 schools were not equally constituted; that is, they differed in size, ability, home environments, class, wealth, etc. The intention was to standardize the interventions across the different schools. However, for a variety of reasons, this was not possible. The main form of comparison, therefore, was not between the different groups but between the different school cohorts at different points of time. The primary focus of the evaluation was on the progress made by the children within their own school during the two years of the project.

The quasi-experimental nature of the design meant that causal relations (i.e. between the intervention and its effects) could not easily be established. Indeed, even if it had been possible to use an experimental design – randomly allocating schools to control and experimental groups and observing the differences – there would still be a number of problems. The first of these is ecological validity – the difficulty of generalizing from the experimental case to other cases in time and place. The second is the need to distinguish between causal relationships and any spurious associations. This evaluation was designed to allow examination of a process – a specific intervention in the 15 schools – and as a result was able to take account of the different ways in which the project was enacted (i.e. the lack of standardization). The programmes being evaluated have powers and potentialities which have been released or partially released in only some of the settings being examined. The purpose of the evaluation was therefore two-fold: first, to examine the actual effects of the programmes during the timespan of the project; and second, to understand the contexts in which they operated.

The stakeholders

There were six stakeholders involved in the evaluation, each with its own vested interests. The first of these was the funding body, The London Docklands Development Corporation, which was accountable to the responsible ministry. It had invested large amounts of money in the project and in the evaluation and was therefore keen to be seen to have invested its money wisely; that is, that the programmes themselves were seen to have raised literacy standards in the Docklands area, whether or not they in fact did. The second stakeholder was the National Literacy Association which managed the project. Though its brief was wider than literacy in the Docklands area, there were similar pressures on it to justify the expenditure of a large sum of money and furthermore to raise the national profile of literacy development throughout the country. Its brief therefore included positive reporting in the specialist and national press of initiatives that it was implementing.

The third stakeholder comprised the designers of the programmes: Global English and Global Mathematics. They were operating within the commercial market and were therefore concerned with its potential saleability. This would be affected by any adverse publicity; indeed, they were keen to encourage favourable reviews of the programmes in action. The fourth stakeholder was the project team itself, which consisted of two ex-teachers and a computer expert, who quickly established relations with the schools which took part in the project, and to some extent, acted in a servicing role to those schools. They were keen for the evaluation to reflect their work and for their work to be seen to be successful, and this included publicizing the effectiveness of the programmes. They were also conscious of being accountable to their funders.

The fifth stakeholder comprised the schools themselves and in particular the teachers who were assigned to deliver the programmes. In some ways they understood the role of the evaluation team as intrusive, in that, though some were convinced of the efficacy of the programmes, they did not see the need for an evaluation of them. In addition, their headteachers had signed a contract with the project team which specified how the programmes should be implemented. They therefore felt themselves to be accountable to their headteachers for this implementation. Their presentations, in the form of giving interviews to the project team, were always structured by this need and the desire to present their school in its best light.

Finally, the evaluation team understood its role as being accountable to the research community in which its members worked. That is, they inevitably made reference to those sets of procedures and epistemological frameworks that underpinned their work as knowledge gatherers, even if they worked in institutions that offered different and in some cases competing paradigms of evaluative knowledge. These six different stakeholders had different vested interests, understood their roles in different ways and sought to influence the contents of the evaluation report in terms of these. The evaluation team, which had ultimate responsibility for the report, had a number of options: to choose one (the most powerful) stakeholder's perspective and to orientate the report so that it conformed to their set of values; to cite a set of academic values that overrode the interests of the other stakeholders; or to attempt a compromise between these different value perspectives.

It was further complicated by the release of the interim report (halfway through the project) to the press, who proceeded to write a highly tendentious and inaccurate account of the findings within it. This satisfied the interests of most of the stakeholders, but clearly transgressed the principles espoused by the evaluation team. Furthermore, it had the effect of putting pressure on the evaluators at an interim stage of their work to produce final results that conformed to the expectations engendered by this newspaper report. In the compilation of the final report, the evaluation team was determined to seek responses from the other stakeholders (in particular, the project team) before publication, and was prepared to make some changes in the light of this new information. In effect, a negotiated compromise was worked out between the different stakeholders, so that as much as possible of each of their agendas was met. However, it would be untrue to suggest that these sets of negotiations were equally framed, since the evaluation team itself conducted the negotiations and ultimately took responsibility for the report. It was also determined to influence press coverage of the report, so that a more accurate account than appeared at the interim stage was presented to the public.

RESEARCH AND EVALUATION

We have examined two of the supposed major differences between evaluation and research: the epistemological assumptions or paradigmatic relations which underpin them and the nature of the settings in which they take place. In the first case, we suggested that the supposed differences between the two rested on certain unfounded assumptions about what research is. If research is thought of as atemporal, asituational, nomothetic and objective (in the traditional sense), then any activity which fails to meet these strict criteria cannot qualify as research. If, on the other hand, research is understood as possibly embracing interpretative perspectives, then the distinction between the two becomes redundant. In the second case, we suggested that evaluators may have to work closely with the many powerful, and in some cases conflicting, agendas which characterize the setting. Researchers, however, cannot avoid issues of power, as these structure the settings that they are investigating, and are a determinant of the data-collection methods they use. This involves a surfacing of this network of power relations and the inscribing of them in the research report (which also involves acts of power).

Even if the distinction which is drawn between evaluation and research seems to be increasingly tenuous conceptually, this has not prevented the establishment of separate disciplinary matrices for each. This has meant that evaluation and research have generally progressed and developed in different ways, though the paucity of the case for describing them as separate activities has meant that, increasingly, practitioners are drawing on both for support and resources, and that methodological approaches have tended to converge.

THIRTEEN
Criteria for Evaluating Research

In this chapter we will examine the various sets of criteria that have been developed by educational researchers to judge the validity of research. Four positions have been suggested (Denzin and Lincoln, 1995). These are:

- *Positivist*: natural science criteria are equally appropriate for the study of the social world. (This is an aparadigmatic perspective.)
- *Post-positivist*: study of the natural and social worlds are such that different criteria are appropriate for each. (This is a di-paradigmatic perspective.)
- *Post-modernist*: no criteria are appropriate for the study of the social world. (This is a multi-perspectival perspective.)
- *Post-structuralist*: new criteria need to be developed which are appropriate for all forms of research. (This is a uni-paradigmatic perspective.)

The first of these, positivism, and its cognate term, empiricism, have been referred to throughout this book. At this point we will provide a summary, though it is important to ensure that this does not amount to a caricaturing of a complex philosophy. Kalakowski (1975) suggests that the model should include four separate elements: phenomenalism, nominalism, a distinction between facts and values, and the unity of the scientific method. The first of these, phenomenalism, refers to the idea that social scientists should only be concerned with surface phenomena and not with underlying essences. Both natural and social scientists should therefore concentrate on how these surface and observable phenomena manifest themselves in regular patterns.

The second element is nominalism. This refers to the belief that the world consists of social and physical facts that cannot be further reduced. The researcher's task is to identify those facts which exist by virtue of what the world is and not because they are perceived or conceived by social actors. They therefore bracket out their value systems and discover what is, and their accounts as a result correspond with that reality in a straightforward way. This has been called naive realism.

The third element separates out factual from value statements and is a logical extension of nominalism. Kalakowski (1975: 13) argues that 'the phenomenalist, nominalist conception of science has another important consequence, namely, the rule that refuses to call value judgements and normative statements knowledge'. An extreme version of this doctrine can be found in the philosophy of logical positivism (cf. Ayer, 1954), advocates of which argue that value-impregnated statements cannot qualify as scientific accounts of the world and that aesthetic, ethical and religious statements are of this order. However, it is possible to make a number of statements about the world, shorn of values, that reflect the world as it is and are not dependent on the personal viewpoint of the knower.

The fourth element is aparadigmatic – natural and social scientific researchers use the same criteria to judge their activities and behave in all essential respects in the same way. This has been called the unity of the scientific method. Method is designated as universal – there is only one correct way of understanding social and natural phenomena.

Positivists–empiricists therefore make law-like or nomothetic statements about the world and their methods allow replicability. These general laws comprise 'the constant conjunction of atomistic events or states of affairs, interpreted as the objects of actual or possible experience' (Bhaskar, 1979: 158). They assume a conflation between ontology (what is) and epistemology (how it can be known) and they therefore can be criticized for adopting what Bhaskar calls the ontic fallacy – i.e. the unjustified conflation of the two.

A number of critiques of positivism–empiricism have been mounted. The first is that data can never be value-free, i.e. free of the conceptions and preconceptions of the researcher; indeed, that the world is known through specific ways of knowing or frameworks. This close relationship between the knower and the known therefore suggests that researchers can never behave as disinterested observers of events. The idea of objective and unitary method becomes untenable. In addition, this naive objectivist position has been challenged from a number of different standpoints. Non-positivists who wish to separate out the textual account of reality from that reality itself would argue that simple correspondence versions of reality fail to come to terms with the complexity of representation. For Macintyre (1988), this applies equally to relativists (there are no rational standards by which we can judge whether one representation is better than another) and perspectivists (here a number of competing and in some cases conflicting accounts are said to be true because the knowers come from different perspectives or are differentially positioned). Furthermore, this weakening of the objectivist position does not mean that it is not possible to adopt a realist position. Bhaskar (1979), for instance, has developed a critical realist position that posits a real world separate from the knower but that can only be captured with extreme difficulty. Any realist position that a researcher chooses to adopt has therefore to take into consideration the inescapable limitations imposed on the researcher by their locatedness in particular discourses, power-plays, environments and time.

The second objection concerns the ability of positivists–empiricists to develop general laws or to be in a position to make nomothetic statements about the world. In order to be able to do this, the researcher has to make a number of assumptions. The first, is that ontology is either stable and intransitive or at least relatively stable – that is, those laws apply to social actors regardless of the circumstances in which they find themselves and these laws have a compelling quality to them. Human beings behave in certain predictable ways. As a result, it is possible to produce prescriptive lists of best possible practice in the social world because these conform to the actual way in which human beings behave and will behave in the future. A second assumption is that epistemology or method is equally stable or intransitive and is not subject to particular social arrangements; that is, power does not enter into the epistemological equation. Foucault (1988) is one philosopher who has attempted to confront this dilemma, which is that social actors adopt different methods at different moments in history and thus this produces different types of truths, which means that social actors understand the world in different ways. He offers the following as one example:

> In the severe world of mental illness, modern man no longer communicates with the madman; or on the other hand, the man of reason delegates the physician to madness, thereby authorizing a relation only through the abstract universality of disease; on the other, the man of madness communicates with society only by the intermediary of an equally abstract reason which is order, physical and moral constraint, the anonymous pressure of the group, the requirements of the conformity. As for a common language, there is no such thing; or rather, there is no such thing any longer; the constitution of madness as mental illness, at the end of the eighteenth century, affords the evidence of a broken dialogue, points the separation as already effected, and thrusts into oblivion all those stammered, imperfect words without fixed syntax in which the exchange between madness and reason was made. (Foucault, 1988: 34)

Foucault's contribution to philosophy is to suggest that these ontological relations between men and women are temporary and in history, and that this applies equally to how they can be known. Another example is provided by Hacking (1990), when he shows that statistical methods are literally an invention of the eighteenth and nineteenth centuries, and their codification as instruments by which reality can be known changes the nature of that reality.

There is a more profound reason for distrusting the ability of researchers to provide nomothetic statements about the world, and this is encapsulated in Giddens's notion of the double hermeneutic. Giddens (1984) argues that there is a profound difference between natural and social science enquiry and this relates to the particular relationship between the constructs developed by social scientists and those used by social actors. These constructs are themselves subject to evaluation and re-evaluation of their worth by social actors acting subsequently, thus changing their original nature. This re-evaluation means that these causal mechanisms inscribed in nomothetic statements about human activity are suddenly no longer simple mechanisms that work on human beings, but now have added to them a further interpretive element. Giddens (1984: 31) is therefore able to argue that this 'introduces an instability into social research' that renders data and their findings problematic:

> The Social Sciences operate with a double hermeneutic involving two-way ties with the actions and institutions of those they study. Sociological observers depend on lay concepts to generate accurate descriptions of social processes; and agents regularly appropriate themes and concepts of social science within their behaviour, thus potentially changing its character. This ... inevitably takes it some distance from the 'cumulative and uncontested' model that naturalistically-inclined sociologists have in mind.

Furthermore, the interpretive element involved in this means that the categories developed by social scientists can only be accurate if they build into their research methodology a self-referential element. In doing this, they create open systems whereby they cannot be sure that the cases they are using to understand social life are in fact the same across time and place.

These are some general remarks about the problems associated with a positivist–empiricist view of research and in particular the criteria used by researchers to judge the effectiveness or otherwise of what they do. These criteria centre on two notions: *internal validity* and *external validity*. The first is a measure of whether in experimentalist terms the effects observed as a result of the intervention have actually been caused by that intervention and not by some other impulsion. The second refers to the ability to generalize from the experimental case to other cases in place and time. We have already made reference in Chapter 5 to the traditional threats to internal validity. To reiterate, these involve history, maturation, pre-test sensitization, test reliability and selection. Threats to external validity relate to: the researcher's need to conceptualize performance indicators; the representativeness of the experimental group with regard to the designated population; the ecological validity of the findings from the experimental group; and the internal validity of the experiment. The distinction between internal and external validity has been criticized by Hammersley (1992), among others, as internally incoherent. He argues that:

> In claiming that the treatment produced the outcome in a particular experiment we are making a causal claim and therefore necessarily implying that in other situations that are similar in relevant respects the same relationship would be found. And if we are investigating such situations and find that the relationship is not present there, and we are confident that this result is not a methodological artifact, we must revise our views about the validity of the

findings of the original experiment. For this reason to talk of different types of validity is misleading. (ibid: 66)

For Hammersley, therefore, if the experimental mode is to be a viable option for researchers, by definition it refers to events and activities which exist outside the experimental setting. However, the fundamental problem is more profound. This is that the representational act implied by such criteria makes a number of epistemological and ontological assumptions in common with the model of positivism described above.

NATURALISTIC INQUIRY

Various alternatives to this have been suggested and these are essentially post-positivist. Because the social world is qualitatively different from the natural world, a different set of criteria is needed. Guba and Lincoln (1985) want to replace traditional criteria such as *internal validity, external validity, reliability* and *objectivity* with different criteria thought appropriate to a post-positivist conception of the world. These are *credibility, transferability, dependability* and *conformability*. These four notions have been criticized because they implicitly assume the same foundational principles of the criteria they were developed to replace. That is, they make the assumption that research is nomological, is objective, is capable of replication and directly represents reality.

Naive realism is the doctrine that language and the texts created from it directly represent in an unproblematic way the world as it is. This has been critiqued both by transcendental realists (cf. Bhaskar, 1989) and by postmodernists (cf. Usher, 1993) for different reasons. Guba and Lincoln (1985) suggest that there are a number of different realities which are equally valid, and their validation rests on whether they are credible to participants in the research. Credibility is a form of respondent validation and rests on the assumption that the participant can have full knowledge of their world. In Chapter 11 we suggested four reasons why this may not be possible. However, there is a further reason for doubting the usefulness of this criterion and this is that the process of validation by respondents always takes place within differentiated settings. Relations of power enter into the way in which respondents validate their reality. However, Guba and Lincoln (1985: 296) suggest that 'the naturalist must show that he or she has represented these multiple constructions adequately, that is, that the reconstructions ... that have been arrived at via the enquiry are credible to the constructors of the original realities'. In order to do this, they argue that researchers, besides using respondent validation techniques, should also use other researchers to check the judgements they make. They should also be aware of disconfirming cases, so that the theory they eventually develop is representative of all the known cases of the phenomena being studied.

The second of Guba and Lincoln's (1985) criteria is transferability. One of the problems with the notion of external validity is that in experimental settings, despite rigorous methodological checks, it is rarely possible to be certain that the artificiality of the case being examined does not impede the making of generalizations or the transposition of the findings of the experimental case to other cases in place and time. Transferability is a looser notion than external validity, in that it places the burden of proof on the reader or user of the research:

> the naturalist cannot specify the external validity of an enquiry; he or she can provide only the thick description necessary to enable someone interested in making a transfer to reach a conclusion about whether the transfer can be contemplated as a possibility. (ibid: 316)

This implies a transparency of method and findings and abandons the idea that the social world can be represented in terms of discrete variables which connect the case being studied to wider populations. Again, it is important to examine the act of reading a text or research report, and understand it as comprising multi-layered and stratified relations of power and knowledge. If this is so, then the only conclusion that can be reached is that it is likely to be read and used in a number of different ways. Since this is presumably what happens anyway, it does not provide a means by which judgements can be made about the validity of the original research.

Guba and Lincoln's (1985) third and fourth notions are those of dependability and confirmability. The social world is such that emergent designs are appropriate for its investigation, whereas pre-determined designs are more appropriate for the study of the natural world, albeit that they can never provide absolute knowledge of events. The problem with emergent designs is that they acknowledge the central role of the researcher in the act of collecting data and thus rule out the possibility of replicability. Guba and Lincoln's solution is to concentrate on the research act itself, and, by using an auditor, posit the notion of an ideal or correct research procedure. The auditor's role is to confirm that the researcher has followed the most appropriate procedures, made the most rational connections between phenomena and drawn the most sensible conclusions that they could have done in the circumstances in which they find themselves. The auditor would have a number of tasks: 'to ascertain whether the findings are grounded in the data ... whether inferences based on the data are logical', whether 'the utility of the category system: its clarity, explanatory power and fit to the data' are realistic, and finally 'the degree and incidence of inquirer bias' (ibid: 318). This criterion masks a number of positions: that the inquirer has developed a definitive method for understanding reality and that intersubjective agreement, which it is suggested is a central principle, can bridge the gap between text and reality. Both researcher and auditor may, of course, agree but both may still be mistaken. Furthermore, the process of achieving intersubjective agreement takes place within definite arrangements of power – they may, for instance, not wish to upset each other.

ALTERNATIVE CRITERIA

Guba and Lincoln (1989) came under fierce attack for grounding their new set of criteria within a positivist perspective or rather for espousing a form of realism, albeit not of a naive kind. Certainly they accepted that their set of criteria was underpinned by the idea of a correct method that would lead to the uncovering of reality and that this concentration on method was at the expense of epistemology and ontology. In an attempt to distance themselves from a positivist–empiricist perspective, Guba and Lincoln (1989) developed a further set of criteria: *fairness* (equal consideration should be given to all the various perspectives of participants in the research); *educative authenticity* (good research involves participants in the process of educating themselves); *catalytic authenticity* (this is where the research process has stimulated activity and decision-making); and *empowerment* (participants are now in a better position to make real choices about their professional activity). This set of criteria focuses on participants and has two major flaws: first, research may empower one set of participants at the expense of another, which means that it is difficult to judge the worth of a project; and second, notions of empowerment and education are ethically neutral, which means that deciding between good and bad accounts is still problematic.

A further set of criteria has been developed by a school of thought known as coherentist realism. Hammersley (1992) and Evers and Lakomski (1991) are leading examples of this school. The last of these argue that:

> Theory choice needs to be guided by a consideration of the extra-empirical virtues possessed by theories. These virtues of system include *simplicity, consistency, coherence, comprehensiveness, conservativeness* and *fecundity*, though they are often referred to collectively as coherence considerations or as elements in a coherentist account of epistemic justification. (ibid: 4)

Scheurich (1997) suggests that there are three major problems with these criteria. First, there is a linguistic problem about how researchers define them. Second, there is a problem of weighting. What if an account is strong in terms of three of these and weak in terms of the other three? Third, there is the problem of them being extra-empirical. In other words, a decisive break has been made between empirical reality and the criteria used to judge accounts of it. As Scheurich (1997: 45) argues: 'If no empirical or rational reasons exist for these coherency criteria, they are historically relative to derivation in particular social or disciplinary contexts (i.e. socially relative).' This does not, of course, mean that they are not useful, but it does mean that they are relative to particular traditions of knowledge and therefore subject to changing social and political arrangements. Hammersley's (1992) four-fold schema of *plausibility/credibility, coherence, intention* and *relevance* has the same instability built into it, and can be critiqued on the grounds that it comprises second-order concepts and that its elements are immersed in history and therefore subject to the controlling influences of those in positions of power.

Finally, therefore, we come to postmodernist critiques. Postmodernism is essentially an attack on foundationalism of all kinds, and, as we suggested at the beginning of this chapter, the search for criteria thought appropriate to the study of the social world founders on the bedrock of the relativity of epistemic knowledge. Thus, naive realism, with its stress on the straightforward relationship between reality and text, and transcendental realism, which emphasizes the irreducibility of events as they are observed to what the world is really like, are guilty of ignoring the transitivity inherent in epistemic arrangements in the first case and ontological relations in the second. However, judgements are made about research texts, including this one, in all sorts of fora. For the postmodernist it is the nature of these judgements which is of concern, rather than the positing of a correct method for their making. Their concern is to understand how these judgements are made, which relations of power they imply and what effects they have. Foucault's (1979) notion of genealogy is directly concerned to do just this: to understand how the assessor, be they policy-maker, university reader or practitioner, is positioned in relation to existing arrangements of power. The next chapter provides a fuller discussion of these issues.

FOURTEEN

Transgressive Research

What is usually highlighted in a postmodern approach to research is a concern with the problematic nature of representation. Related to this is the issue of interruption or disruption mentioned in Chapter 2. But an interruption or disruption of what? Perhaps we can say of 'closure' in the same way as we might of 'certainty' or of 'validity' that it implies that research is 'well-grounded'. This has a bearing on the problem of how difficult it is to say what a postmodern approach is. In some ways, it is easier to say what it is not – it is not another paradigm or another methodology, let alone a new tool-kit for doing research. All that can be safely said about it is that it offers a way of resisting closure and possibilities for 'opening up' the research process, allowing us to ask the question – what is going on when we do research?

Yet the very asking of this question poses certain dangers, since any 'opening up' can mean falling into the abyss so opened of relativism and nihilism. To argue, as Stronach and MacLure (1997) do, that in the field of education a postmodern approach can function to make educational research *unfamiliar*, startling in itself though this thought may be, seems unimportant compared to the possibility of falling into chaos and uncertainty, which a resistance to closure might imply. At the very least, then, any process of 'opening up' must involve some commitment to living with uncertainty and thus would require accepting its dangers as well as its possibilities. At the same time it could be argued that the dangers of falling into this abyss are vastly exaggerated in three possible ways – first, there is no danger, second, there is no abyss, and third, relativism is in any event a modernist trick. As Burbules and Rice (1991) argue, postmodernism is about reappropriating and redefining modernist categories, and included in this would be relativism itself. In this sense, postmodernism is not setting itself up as a superordinate truth but rather challenging modernist epistemology to recognize its own relativistic character and its silence on issues of knowledge and power. What is being argued for here is what Scheurich (1997) refers to as 'social relativism' – a position which argues that epistemology is itself historically and culturally relative and hence there can be no foundational truth claims.

This is why it is possible to argue against a commonly accepted criticism that postmodernism, because of its relativistic tendencies, has nothing to say of an ethical nature. Critics argue that because it provides no common standard which cuts across the multiplicity of discourses there would seem to be no way of making ethical judgements about particular discourses, including different research discourses – in effect, each would seem to be as good as any other. Taking a position of *social* relativism however – that there are always social and historical constraints, themselves contestable, on what is allowed – takes care of the nihilistic implications of the 'anything goes' argument. But this is not the whole story, since this criticism is sometimes also framed as postmodernism being more concerned with aesthetics (or style) than with ethics. Now in some ways this is undoubtedly the case, since there is a concern with the way in which research texts are written and how meanings are organized by essentially literary means – the intersection of the academic and the literary mentioned in an earlier chapter. The reflexivity inherent in the notion of 'text' demands that attention be paid to the textuality of research, so how the text is written is just as important as what it is about. There is also a sense in which the aesthetic emphasis can serve as a kind of 'subversion' of the text, the means to opening up resistance to closure.

However, conceiving the aesthetic emphasis as problematic is rooted in the binary opposition 'ethics–aesthetics' through which this critique is conducted. Yet deconstructively it could be argued that the aesthetic and the ethical cannot be separated in this polarized way and with the latter always privileged over the former and that, on the contrary, the aesthetic is also ethical and ethics must necessarily have an aesthetic dimension. This means that postmodernism, in emphasizing the aesthetic, is not merely reversing traditional hierarchical binaries for the sake of subversive play but is actually constructing itself as an *ethical* enterprise. The implications of this are that a postmodern approach necessarily involves ethical issues as integral to the research process. It means seeing research, whichever paradigm it is carried out in, as being just as much about values – values of anti-universalism, anti-transcendentalism, privileging the marginalized and the silenced – as it is about methods and outcomes, and it is to see ethical issues, whether acknowledged or unacknowledged, as immanent in any process of knowledge production. The postmodern critique of the universalizing thrust of Western philosophy, its need to operate within an economy of the same, is not accompanied by the construction of its own equally oppressive alternative. As Elam (1994) argues, there are no more transcendental alibis for us to fall back on, no essences which will save us from the need to judge on a case-by-case basis. A postmodern approach to research does not seek to overthrow and replace existing research paradigms and traditions but it does seek to critique them and to thus call attention to aspects which are neglected or ignored. The place of ethics as immanent rather than purely procedural also provides a different way of understanding the research process – a way which foregrounds the need to be aware of the relationship between researchers, knowledge and power where an emphasis on reflexivity is not simply another technique but a reminder that research is never a purely technical process.

At this point, however, we run into different problems, for there is a need to consider not only postmodernism and its implications for research but also postmodernity or what Lyotard (1984) has termed the 'postmodern condition'. Once we do this we find that what tends to be present is a situation where 'performativity' is rapidly assuming a dominant place – and with that bringing all kinds of disturbing implications for research. Put very simply, performativity is neatly summed up by this remark – 'we don't want to know whether our research is right or wrong. If it works for our clients, that's the bottom line for us.' At the very least, performativity and its demands do not appear to offer much scope for an ethical dimension.

It is probably worth saying a little at this point about how Lyotard understands performativity. He traces its growth to the fundamental problem that we discussed earlier of establishing the validity of research outcomes, or to put it very simply – how is proof to be proven? There are two aspects to this. The first is that to simply describe how a proof is obtained has never been enough, since given the realist metaphysic it is 'reality' itself that must provide definitive evidence before something can be accepted as proven. Historically, this problem has been resolved by limiting proof to certain kinds of repeatable observations, immune to the deceptiveness and limitations of the senses – Lather's 'incitement to see'. It is here that technology comes into the picture, for it has the capacity to optimize the performance of the human body for 'seeing' and thus enhancing the validity of observations. With technology enabling reality to be mastered, science (research) and technology become inter-related and inseparable. Something significantly different is added to research by this, since it is no longer oriented to truth but to technology's imperative of efficiency and optimal performance. Furthermore, the dependence on technology means in turn a dependence on funding, since technology requires money. The combination of emphasizing optimal performance and the need for money made a marriage between research, the economic order and the state almost inevitable – with research becoming implicated with power at the macro- as well as the micro-level. Second, Lyotard argues that science-based knowledge depends for its legitimacy not so much on epistemologically defined methods and rules as on cultural attitudes. The culture of modernity is characterized by grand narratives about the value and truth of science and of truth itself but once, as in postmodernity, these grand narratives are viewed with incredulity, then so too is the legitimacy of knowledge. Basically, science and its knowledge cannot legitimate itself – it needs non-science, epic stories of inevitable progress and human betterment through scientific knowledge to legitimate it. With the breakdown of legitimacy, what counts as knowledge is itself reconfigured, and therefore the activity of knowledge production itself assumes a different legitimacy. The outcome of all this is that one (although not the only) feature of the postmodern condition is what Lyotard describes as 'the generalized spirit of performativity'. He talks of a contemporary self-legitimation by power: power is good performativity, and it legitimates research on the basis of its efficiency and legitimates this efficiency on the basis of research.

Picking up, therefore, on the earlier point, the problem we are faced with is that, on the one hand, we have foregrounded the ethical dimension (and, earlier, the political dimension) as significant in a postmodern approach to research, and, on the other hand, we have now just acknowledged the power–performativity dimension within research in conditions of postmodernity. At one level, performativity is antithetical to what we have characterized as the postmodern approach to research, in that it tends towards reducing difference, to ignoring that which cannot be assimilated to the same and to treating all language as commensurable – commensurable, that is, to optimizing the system's overall performance. The question now is – given the generally constrained conditions for research in the contemporary period, which the emphasis on performativity has itself contributed to – is it possible or indeed necessary for research to escape its demands? A postmodern approach, as we have seen, regards traditional notions of validity as suspect – as the oppressive expression of a regime of truth. One can put this very starkly – what does validity mean in a situation where an equally oppressive regime of performativity is becoming increasingly dominant? Is it then possible to reconfigure validity in a way which, whilst recognizing its locatedness in the contemporary regime, still allows some space for resisting its more oppressive features? One possible way forward lies in the notion of transgressive validity. As we have seen earlier, Lather (1994) characterizes her version of transgressive validity as a *counter-practice of authority*, challenging validity as a regime of truth by running counter to a validity of correspondence. So, in this sense, a transgressive perspective on validity is not concerned with how research methodologies work but with how they very often *fail* to work.

The current research economy, with its emphasis on performativity, is subject to a number of tensions which have methodological, epistemological and political consequences. The state-sponsored demands of performativity has meant that the spaces of educational research have been compressed and politically moulded, and this is manifested in such things as intensification of research work through shorter contracts, greater formal control by state and quasi-state bodies, job insecurity of research workers and greater links between policy and research (Stronach and MacLure, 1997). They argue that all this has affected every mainstream research paradigm in which specific research has traditionally been located. These paradigms are being played out in different milieux, where their key concepts are still deployed but at the same time transformed. They characterize this development in terms of three 'games' of research. In game 1, research is lengthy, theory-oriented, experiential (fieldwork oriented), and belongs to a recognized research paradigm embodying all the modernistic assumptions about knowledge, an essentialist view of the researcher, e.g. as ethnographer, and the need for a lengthy research apprenticeship. The contextual changes brought about by postmodernity have affected the rationalization and conduct of research and have brought about a movement from game 1 to another game, game 2, characterized by fragmentation in research, short projects and abridged methods, and subject to strong political pressures.

All this has methodological implications. Researchers professionally socialized into game 1 have attempted to adapt their practice to the new context and conditions and now play game 2. This is a kind of 'short-cut' research, which Stronach and MacLure characterize as involving legitimizing citations of the methodological masters but not the realization of the implied practices. They argue that in this game methodology becomes part of a culture of quotation and name-dropping, although researchers in game 2 do at least have a grounding in game 1 from which to orchestrate their game 2 compromises. Once this grounding disappears, however, researchers are into the performative game 3, with its characteristics of the business ethos, the decline of traditional research cultures, of 'hit and run projects', and of a speed and fragmentation of work that leaves them isolated and vulnerable. Given, then, the increasing prevalence of game 3 research, the question that emerges is how this development is to be understood – as entirely negative or in a counter-intuitive way as productive of positive possibilities?

Stronach and MacLure take the view that there might well be something positive. They pose the question – how can a different validity be constructed on the back of the ruins of classic methodology? They believed that it might be possible to construct such a validity from a different kind of 'negotiation' between them and their research subjects, and they exemplify this in a short-term, small-scale evaluation project which, by its very nature, required improvisations and short-cuts and a tight time-frame – in other words, it had many of the features of game 3 research. The question then was – how are these features to be understood? Simply as the triumph of performativity and therefore in a negative way or as productive of more positive possibilities?

The research used a questionnaire designed to provide feedback on a preliminary data analysis based on semi-structured interviews; however, it was designed as a series of summary statements about a training programme that respondents had taken part in so as to invite them to agree, disagree and add to the feedback in whatever way they wished. From the responses, the researchers were able to elicit a number of categories of response on a transgressive–non-transgressive dimension. Respondents' interventions were regarded as minimally transgressive where responses were expressed formally and in conformity with the rubric of the instrument. More active interventions involved qualifications or additions, perhaps unconventionally located in a margin or extemporized with an asterisk, or informally or emphatically expressed. The strongest interventions in the transgressive sense were those that involved a challenge to the rubrics of response (refusal to tick or cross, scoring out, criticizing the format). There was also an unexpected category of response referred to as implicit dialogue that included the raising of non-rhetorical questions, citation of individuals who had done well on the course, and asking researchers to get in touch for more information – all of which the researchers considered expressions of interactivity and negotiation.

Stronach and MacLure report that the procedure succeeded in provoking a kind of dialogue and negotiation whose interactivity was transgressive in relation to the classic formal procedures of the questionnaire. Of course, it could be argued that most questionnaires have an 'anything to add' invitation anyway – but the difference here was that this was deliberately foregrounded. A disobeying by respondents of the protocols of the questionnaire would conventionally be considered a mark of deficient validity but here it was the very *disobedience* which constituted validity. They argue that this research was characterized by its hybrid nature; for example, it was both a questionnaire and interim report, and it treated respondents as audience and informants, inviting them to disagree with both the form and the substance of the questionnaire. Furthermore, there was a multiple hybridity – as narrative (both report and inquiry), as both validating and invalidating its methods of knowledge construction, and as a transgressive validity that used rather than rejected rival warrants. At the same time, however, there was no 'anything goes' approach – in other words, no abdication of methodological responsibility.

As Stronach and MacLure point out, all this has implications for traditional notions of negotiation and dialogue considered so important in educational research. Given that negotiation is about changing the power–knowledge relationship inherent in research, the interactions between researcher and researched in this research were made less asymmetrical in terms of power through enabling the latter to be more actively engaged in the research process. Negotiation was not simply *post hoc* or a preliminary to fieldwork but at the heart of the research process where knowledge was being produced. There was an incitement for the respondents to disobey the research instrument, contradict preliminary findings, argue with the method, and dispute the implied register of response – all of which could be construed as 'negotiation'. Here, then, negotiation therefore became 'rules' for *inciting* rather than settling disputes – an incitement located in practitioners rather than stakeholders. Much of this was undoubtedly due to the postmodern interest of the researchers in the interaction between the respondents' and the researchers' texts, and the informal re-writing by the respondents of the researchers' text.

All this raises an interesting point. We started by highlighting changes in the conduct and aims of research through the demands of performativity as an aspect of the postmodern condition, whereas now we can see hybrid research as reflecting something of the loose coupling or flexibility which is the other side of the same condition. This may have certain advantages, since it could be argued that the emphasis in game 1 research on methodological purity, set rubrics of enquiry and report, implied registers of response, and prior specification of relevance, were themselves inherent in the regimes of power and truth they were researching. Thus the scope for critique in game 1 research was always limited. This would seem to suggest that the purity of methodologies was compromised even in game 1 research and certainly in game 2 research. What Stronach and MacLure are reporting is a hybrid research that involves not a rejection of existing methodologies but rather an acknowledgement of their transgressive 'other'. The notion of 'hybrid research' embodies an 'in-betweenness' that recognizes yet also resists closure. In this way, game 3 research can be seen as not so much a complete break of a postmodern from a modernist approach but perhaps rather a reconfiguration of the necessary relationship between the two.

At this point, however, it might not be unreasonable to question the significance of transgressive validity and hybrid research. We can probably accept that hybrid research as Stronach and MacLure describe it has transgressive elements, yet we cannot help but ask whether it amounts to very much. On the face of it, it does seem rather insignificant, hardly likely to change the world. However, perhaps it is necessary to recall what Stronach and MacLure were trying to do – to show not only that performativity could be resisted but also how this resistance cannot take the form of a return to the golden days of game 1 research. Instead, it almost inevitably had to take the form of hybrid research with a transgressive validity – a form which recognizes the existence of the conditions of game 3 research but, rather than accept these conditions passively and completely, seeks also to do something different and subversive. In other words, research becomes a playing of the game whilst simultaneously subverting it.

The achievement may be small but at the very least it is certainly not something that game 1, let alone game 2, could ever achieve. What it emphasizes is that a resistant practice of research needs to be located in the local and the specific, where interventions are defined situationally and participatorily (Lather, 1994). This is why a postmodern approach to research offers no alternative or all-encompassing methodology, and recognizes the limits of its empowering potential. But it does acknowledge that, although closure may be a fate, it is a fate to be resisted. Texts are doubly coded in that they offer the hybridity of both complicity and critique. And this, it could be argued, gets us back to ethics and politics despite, or maybe because of, the demands of performativity.

On the face of it, it is odd that despite its location in the postmodern condition, performativity appears to be the most contemporary form taken by foundation-alism, the latest version of the desire for closure and presence, for the 'given' of an authorizing centre, in this case that of optimal efficiency. There is also an irony here, given the roots of game 1 research in the realist metaphysic, for those who bemoan its fate under the constraints of performativity. Realism posits the independent objectivity of the world knoweable through scientific research, knowledge thus being the accurate representation of that world. This knowledge is seen as linear, cumulative, and progressive in its application – with research therefore producing 'useful' knowledge through 'relevant' research addressed to 'real-world' problems. This knowledge is produced by standing apart from the world in the cause of objectivity but assuming the right to intervene in it in the cause of resolving those problems. Earlier we discussed how performativity is associated with a delegitimation and reconfiguration of knowledge. It is one of the characteristics of the postmodern condition that the real and its representation can no longer be so clearly distinguished. On the one hand, the mediated and simulated culture of the postmodern tends to make everything a representation detached from the real, whilst on the other, the questioning of grand narratives that delegitimates knowledge has, as Lemert (1997) points out, also cast into doubt the supposed nature of the real assumed by traditionally legitimated knowledge. When knowledge is no longer so secure, neither is reality. Performativity could thus be seen as an attempt to reconfigure reality, giving it a different kind of security, through reconfiguring knowledge as that which optimizes efficiency. In a sense, contemporary performativity in research is none other than a reassertion of the realist metaphysic – the return of that which realism has repressed. In other words, realism has always been about performativity – it is just out in the open now, stripped of the metaphysical language.

However, having said this, it is also important not to understand performativity in too gloomy a light. There is a difference now which is also to be found in the social and cultural changes that we have referred to as the postmodern condition. These changes mean that it has become increasingly difficult to engage in closure – to arrest meanings in a world characterized by the mobility of meanings and to fix their uncertain trajectories. When knowledge is delegitimated, when it is no longer so closely bounded and patrolled by the epistemological police, what takes its place is an 'un-ruliness' of knowledge which even performativity cannot halt – which indeed performativity by its boundary-breaking and disregard for the traditional canons of research actually helps to bring about. Thus performativity cannot ever be foundational in a modernist sense. It is the very 'unrul-iness' which it stimulates that provides the scope for resistant practices of research – even against itself.

References

Archer, M. (1982) 'Morphogenesis versus Structuration', *British Journal of Sociology*, 33(4): 455–83.

Archer, M. (1988) *Culture and Agency*, Cambridge: Cambridge University Press.

Ayer, A.J. (1954) *Knowledge, Truth and Logic*, London: Gollancz.

Ball, S. and Goodson, I. (eds) (1985) *Teachers' Lives and Careers*, Lewes: Falmer Press.

Barthes, R. (1975) *The Semiotic Challenge*, New York: Hill and Wang.

Bartlett, D. and Payne, S. (1997) 'Grounded Theory – Its Basis, Rationale and Procedures', in G. McKenzie, J. Powell and R. Usher (eds) *Understanding Social Research: Perspectives on Methodology and Practice*, Lewes: Falmer Press.

Becker, H. (1966) 'Introduction', in C. Show, *The Jack Roller*, Chicago: Chicago University Press.

Bernstein, B. (1971) 'On the Classification and Framing of Educational Knowledge', in M. Young (ed.) *Knowledge and Control*, London: Collier-Macmillan.

Bhabha, H. (1994) *The Location of Culture*, London: Routledge.

Bhaskar, R. (1979) *The Possibility of Naturalism*, Brighton: Harvester Press.

Bhaskar, R. (1989) *Reclaiming Reality*, London: Verso.

Bhaskar, R. (1993) *Dialectic: The Pulse of Freedom*, London: Verso.

Blaikie, N. (1993) *Approaches to Social Enquiry*, Cambridge: Polity Press.

Bleicher, J. (1982) *The Hermeneutic Imagination*, London: Routledge and Kegan Paul.

Blumer, H. (1969) *Symbolic Interactionism*, Englewood Cliffs, New Jersey: Prentice Hall.

Bohman, J. (1991) *New Philosophy of Social Science*, Oxford: Polity Press.

Bryant, I. (1996) 'Action Research and Reflective Practice', in D. Scott and R. Usher (eds) *Understanding Educational Research*, London: Routledge.

Bryant, I. and Jones, K. (1995) *Quantitative Methods and Statistical Processes in Educational Research*, University of Southampton.

Bryman, A. (1988) *Quality and Quantity in Social Research*, London: Unwin and Hyman.

Bulmer, M. (1979) 'Concepts in the Analysis of Qualitative Data', *Sociological Review*, 27(4): 651–77.

Burbules, N. and Rice, R. (1991) 'Dialogues Across Difference; Continuing the Conversation', *Harvard Educational Review*, 61(4): 393–416.

Burgess, R.G. (1984) *In the Field: An Introduction to Field Research*, London: Allen and Unwin.

Burgess, R.G. (1986) *Sociology, Education and Schools: An Introduction to the Sociology of Education*, London: B.T. Batsford Ltd.

Campbell, D.T. and Stanley, J.C. (1963) 'Experimental and Quasi-experimental Designs for Research on Teaching', in N. Gage (ed.) *Handbook of Research on Teaching*, Chicago: Rand McNally.

Carr, W. and Kemmis, S. (1986) *Becoming Critical: Education, Knowledge and Action Research*, Lewes: Falmer.

Cherryholmes, C. (1988) 'An Exploration of Meaning and the Dialogue between Textbooks and Teaching', *Journal of Curriculum Studies*, 20(1): 1–21.

Clifford, J. and Marcus, G. (1986) *Writing Culture: The Poetics and Politics of Ethnography*, Berkeley: University of California Press.

Cohen, L. and Manion, L. (1989) *Research Methods in Education*, 3rd edn, London: Routledge.

Crapanzano, V. (1986) 'Hermes Dilemma: the Masking of Subversion in Ethnographic Description', in J. Clifford and G. Marcus (1986) *Writing Culture: The Poetics and Politics of Ethnography*, Berkeley: University of California Press.

Creemens, B. and Scheerens, J. (eds) (1989) 'Development in School Effectiveness Research', *International Journal of Education Research*, Special Edition, 13: 685–825.

Denzin, N. (1989a) *Interpretive Interactionism*, Vol. 16, Applied Social Research Methods, London: Sage.

Denzin, N. (1989b) *Interpretive Biography*, Beverley Hills, CA: Sage Publications.

Denzin, N. and Lincoln, Y. (eds) (1995) *Handbook of Qualitative Research*, London: Sage.

Derrida, J. (1978) *Writing and Difference*, Chicago: University of Chicago Press.

Descartes, R. (1949) (translated by John Veitch) *A Discourse on Method*, London: J.M. Dent.

Dickinson, H. (1994) 'Narratives in the Experience of Learning Difficulties', *Auto/Biography*, 3, 2: 93–104.

Dunne, J. (1993) *Back to the Rough Ground*, London: University of Notre Dame Press.

Ebbutt, D. (1985) 'Educational Action Research: Some General Concerns and Specific Possibilities', in R.G. Burgess (ed.) *Issues in Qualitative Research: Qualitative Methods*, Lewes: Falmer Press.

Eckstein, H. (1975) 'Case Study and Theory in Political Science', in F. Greenstein and N. Polsby (eds) *Strategies of Inquiry: Handbook of Political Science*, 7, Menlo Park, California: Addison-Wesley.

Eisner, E.W. (1975) 'Applying Educational Connoisseurship and Criticism to Education Settings', in D. Hamilton, D. Jenkins, C. King, B. MacDonald and M. Parlett (eds) (1977) *Beyond the Numbers Game: A Reader in Educational Evaluation*, London: Macmillan.

Elam, D. (1994) Feminism and Deconstruction, London: Routledge.

Elliott, J. (1983) 'Self-Evaluation, Professional Development and Accountability', in M. Galton and B. Moon (eds) *Changing Schools . . . Changing Curriculum*, London: Harper and Row.

Elliott, J. (1991) *Action Research for Educational Change*, Milton Keynes: Open University Press.

Elverno, J., Greenwood, D., Martin, A., Mathews, L., Strubel, A., Thomas, L. and Whyte, W. (1997) 'Participation, Action and Research in the Classroom', *Studies in Continuing Education*, 19(1): 1–50.

Elwood, J. (1996) 'Undermining Gender Stereotypes: Examination and Coursework Performance in the UK at 16', *Assessment in Education*, 2(3): 283–303.

Erben, M. (1996) 'The Purposes and Processes of Biographical Method', in D. Scott and R. Usher (eds) *Understanding Educational Research*, London: Routledge.

Evers, C. and Lakomski, G. (1991) *Knowing Educational Administration: Contemporary Methodological Controversies in Educational Administration*, Oxford: Pergamon Press.

Fairclough, N. (1992) *Language and Power*, London and New York: Longman

Feyerabend, P. (1993) *Against Method*, London: Verso.

Fielding, N. (1981) *The National Front*, London: Routledge and Kegan Paul.

Fine, M. (1994) 'Dis-stance and other stances: Negotiations of Power inside Feminist Research', in A. Gitlin (ed.) *Power and Method*, London: Routledge.

Flanders, N. (1970) *Analysing Teaching Behaviours*, New York: Addison-Wesley.

Foucault, M. (1979) *Discipline and Punish: The Birth of the Prison*, New York: Vintage.

Foucault, M. (1980) *Power/Knowledge*, Brighton: Harvester Press.

Foucault, M. (1988) *Madness and Civilization: A History of Insanity in the Age of Reason*, New York: Vintage.

Gadamer, H-G. (1975) *Truth and Method*, London: Sheed and Ward.

Galton, M., Simon, B. and Croll, P. (1980) *Inside the Primary Classroom*, London: Routledge and Kegan Paul.

Geertz, C. (1973) *The Interpretation of Cultures*, New York: Basic Books.

Giddens, A. (1976) *New Rules of Sociological Method*, London: Hutchinson.

Giddens, A. (1984) *The Constitution of Society*, Cambridge: Polity Press.

Gillborn, D. and Gipps, C. (1996) *Recent Research on the Achievements of Ethnic Minority Pupils*, London: OFSTED.

Gipps, C. (1994) *Beyond Testing: Towards a Theory of Educational Assessment*, London: Falmer Press.

Gipps, C. and Murphy, P. (1995) *A Fair Test? Assessment and Equity*, Buckingham: Open University Press.

Gitlin, A. and Russell, R. (1994) 'Alternative Methodologies and the Research

Context', in A. Gitlin (ed.) *Power and Method*, London: Routledge.

Glaser, B. and Strauss, A. (1967) *The Discovery of Grounded Theory: Strategies for Qualitative Research*, London: Weidenfeld and Nicolson.

Glass, G. and Worthen, B. (1971) 'Evaluation and Research: Similarities and Differences', *Curriculum Theory Network*, Fall, 149–65.

Gold, R. (1958) 'Roles in Sociological Fieldwork', *Social Forces*, 36: 217–23.

Goldstein, H. (1987) *Multilevel Models in Education and Social Research*, Oxford: Clarendon Press.

Goodson, I. (1985) 'History, Context and Qualitative Methods in the Study of the Curriculum', in R. Burgess (ed.) *Strategies of Educational Research: Qualitative Methods*, Lewes: Falmer Press.

Gore, J. (1993) *The Struggle for Pedagogies*, London: Routledge.

Guba, E. and Lincoln, Y. (1981) *Effective Evaluation*, San Francisco, CA: Jossey Bass.

Guba, E. and Lincoln, Y. (1985) *Naturalistic Enquiry*, London: Sage.

Guba, E. and Lincoln, Y. (1989) *Fourth Generation Evaluation*, London: Sage.

Habermas, J. (1987) *Knowledge and Human Interests*, Cambridge: Polity Press.

Hacking, I. (1990) *The Taming of Chance*, Cambridge: Cambridge University Press.

Hage, J. and Meeker, B. (1993) 'How to Think About Causality', in M. Hammersley (ed.) *Educational Research: Current Issues*, London: Paul Chapman Publishing Ltd.

Hammersley, M. (1992) *What's Wrong with Ethnography?* London: Routledge.

Hammersley, M. and Atkinson, P. (1983) *Ethnography: Principles in Practice*, London and New York: Tavistock Publications.

Haraway, D. (1991) *Simians, Cyborgs and Women: The Reinvention of Nature*, London: Free Association Books.

Hargreaves, D.H. (1972) *Interpersonal Relations and Education*, London: Routledge and Kegan Paul.

Harré, R. (1961) *Theories and Things*, London: Sheed and Ward.

Harré, R. (1972) *The Philosophies of Science*, Oxford: Oxford University Press.

Heidegger, M. (1962) *Being and Time*, Oxford: Basil Blackwell.

Heyes, S., Hardy, M., Humphreys, P. and Rookes, P. (1993) *Starting Statistics in Psychology and Education*, 2nd edn, London: Croom Helm.

Hitchcock, G. and Hughes, D. (1989) *Research and the Teacher: A Qualitative Introduction to School-based Research*, London: Routledge.

Hockey, J. (1991) *Squaddies*, Exeter: Exeter University Press.

Hollinger, R. (1994) *Postmodernism and the Social Sciences*, London: Sage.

Hume, D. (1739) *Enquiry Concerning Human Understanding*, Oxford: Selby-Bigge.

Husserl, E. (1960) *Cartesian Meditations: An Introduction to Phenomenology* (translated By Dorion Cairns), The Hague: Nijhoff.

Kolakowski, L. (1975) *Husserl and the Search for Certitude*, New Haven: Yale University Press.

Keat, R. and Urry, J. (1975) *Social Theory as Science*, London: Routledge and Kegan Paul.

Kelly, E. (1975) 'Curriculum Evaluation and Literary Criticism: Comments on the Analogy', *Curriculum Theory Network*, 5: 98–106.

Kuhn, T. (1970) *The Structure of Scientific Revolutions*, Chicago: University of Chicago Press.

Lather, P. (1986) 'Research as Praxis', *Harvard Educational Review*, 56(3): 257–77.

Lather, P. (1991) *Getting Smart: Feminist Research and Pedagogy with/in the Postmodern*, New York: Routledge.

Lather, P. (1994) 'Fertile Obsession: Validity after Poststructuralism', in A. Gitlin (ed.) *Power and Method*, London: Routledge.

Layder, D. (1993) *New Strategies in Social Research*, Cambridge: Polity Press.

Leitch, V. (1996) *Postmodernism: Local Effects, Global Flows*, Albany: SUNY Press.

Lemert, C. (1997) *Postmodernism is Not What You Think*, Oxford: Blackwell.

Levine, D. (1992) 'An Interpretive Review of US Research and Practice Dealing with Unusual Effective Schools', in D. Reynolds and P. Cuttance (eds) *School Effectiveness Research, Policy and Practice*, London: Cassell.

Lofland, J. and Lofland, L. (1984) *Analysing Social Settings: a Guide to Qualitative Observation and Analysis*, Belmont, California: Wadsworth.

Lyotard, J-F. (1984) *The Postmodern Condition: A Report on Knowledge*, Manchester: Manchester University Press.

MacDonald, B. (1974) 'Evaluation and the Control of Education', in B. MacDonald and R. Walker (eds) *SAFARI 1: Innovation, Evaluation, Research and the Problem of Control*, Norwich: Centre for Applied Research in Education, University of East Anglia.

Macintyre, A. (1988) *Whose Justice? Which Rationality?* London: Duckworth.

Mann, C. (1994) 'How Did I Get to Here? Educational Life Histories of Adolescent Girls Doing A Levels', *Auto/Biography*, 3, 2: 59–70.

Marx, K. (1976) *Capital*, Vol. 1, Harmondsworth: Penguin.

McClaren, P. (1995) *Critical Pedagogy and Predatory Culture*, London and New York: Routledge.

Measor, L. and Woods, P. (1983) *Changing Schools*, Milton Keynes: Open University Press.

Merton, R.K. (1957) *Social Theory and Social Structure*, Chicago: Free Press

Miles, M. and Huberman, M. (1984), *Qualitative Data Analysis*, Beverley Hills: Sage.

Mitchell, J.C. (1983) 'Case Study and Situational Analysis', *Sociological Review*, 31(2): 187–211.

Mortimore, P. (1992) 'Issues in School Effectiveness', in D. Reynolds and P. Cuttance (eds) *School Effectiveness Research, Policy and Practice*, London: Cassell.

Mortimore, P. and Sammons, P. (1997) 'Endpiece: A Welcome and Riposte to Critics', in M. Barber and J. White (eds) *Perspectives on School Effectiveness and School Improvement*, Bedford Way Papers, London Institute of Education.

Mortimore, P., Sammons, P., Stoll, L., Lewis, D. and Ecob, R. (1988) *School Matters: The Junior Years*, Wells: Open Books.

Moseley, D. (1995) *Access to Literacy with Global English, Part 1*. University of Newcastle-Upon-Tyne.

Moser, C. and Kalton, G. (1977) *Survey Methods in Social Investigation*, London: Heinemann.

Norris, N. (1992) *Understanding Educational Evaluation*, London: Kogan Page.

Nuttall, D. (1987) 'The Validity of Assessments', *European Journal of Psychology of Education*, 11(2): 109–18.

Pagano, R. (1990) *Understanding Statistics in the Behavioural Sciences*, 3rd edn, London: West Publishing.

Parker, S. (1997) *Reflective Teaching in a Postmodern World*. Buckingham: Open University Press.

Parsons, T. (1964) *Social Structure and Personality*, New York: Free Press.

Partlett, M. and Hamilton, D. (1972) 'Evaluation as Illumination: a New Approach to the Study of Innovatory Programmes', *Occasional Paper 9*, Centre for Research in the Educational Sciences, University of Edinburgh.

Pawson, R. and Tilley, N. (1997) *Realistic Evaluation*, London: Sage Publications.

Phtiaka, H. (1997) *Special Kids for Special Treatment*, Lewes: Falmer Press.

Popper, K. (1976) 'The Logic of the Social Sciences', in T. Adorno, R. Albert, R. Dahrendorf, J. Habermas, H. Pilot and K. Popper (eds) *The Positivist Dispute in German Sociology*, London: Heinemann.

Reinharz, S. (1992) *Feminist Methods in Social Research*, New York and Oxford: Oxford University Press.

Rippey, R. (ed.) (1973) *Studies in Transactional Evaluation*, Berkeley CA: McCutchan.

Robson, C. (1993) *Real World Research: A Resource for Social Scientists and Practitioner-Researchers*, Oxford: Blackwell.

Rorty, R. (1980) *Philosophy and the Mirror of Nature*, Oxford: Blackwell.

Rudduck, J. (1991) *Innovation and Change*, Milton Keynes: Open University Press.

Sammons, P., Hillman, J. and Mortimore, P. (1995) *Key Characteristics of Effectiveness: a Review of School Effectiveness Research*, London: Office for Standards in Education.

Sammons, P., Thomas, S. and Mortimore, P. (1997) *Forging Links: Effective Schools and Effective Departments*, London: Paul Chapman Publishing Ltd.

Sanday, A. (1990) *Making Schools more Effective* (CEDAR Papers 2), Centre for Educational Development, Appraisal and Research, University of Warwick.

Sayer, A. (1992) *Method in Social Science*, London: Routledge.

Scheurich, J. (1997) *Research Method in the Postmodern*, Lewes: Falmer Press.

Schutz, A. (1963) 'Common-sense and Scientific Interpretation of Human Action', in M. Natanson (ed.) *Philosophy of the Social Sciences*, New York: Random House.

Schutz, A. (1964) 'The Stranger: An Essay in Social Psychology', in A. Schutz (ed.) *Collected Papers,* Vol. 1, The Hague: Martinus Nijhoff.

Schutz, A. (1967) (ed. M. Natanson) *Collected Papers*, Vol. 2, The Hague: Martinus Nijhoff.

Schwandt, T. (1994) 'Constructivist, Interpretivist Approaches to Human Inquiry', in N. Denzin and Y. Lincoln (eds) *Handbook of Qualitative Research*, London: Sage.

Scott, D. (1992) *Career Aspirations and Educational Experiences of 16–30 Year Old Afro-Caribbeans*, Coventry: University of Warwick.

Scott, D. (1997a) 'The Missing Hermeneutical Dimension in School Effectiveness Research', in M. Barber and J. White (eds) *School Effectiveness Research and its Critics*, Bedford Way Paper, London Institute of Education.

Scott, D. (1997b) 'Qualitative Approaches to Data Collection and Analysis: Examinations and Schools', in G. McKenzie, J. Powell and R. Usher (eds) *Understanding Social Research: Perspectives on Methodology and Practice*, Lewes: Falmer Press.

Scott, D. (1998a) 'Approaches to Evaluating Health Promotion', in D. Scott and R. Weston (eds) *Evaluating Health Promotion*, London: Chapman and Hall.

Scott, D. (1998b) 'Ethics and Evaluation', in D. Scott and R. Weston (eds) *Evaluating Health Promotion*, London: Chapman and Hall.

Scott, D. (1998c) 'Fragments of a Life: Recursive Dilemmas', in M. Erben (ed.) *Education and Biography: A Book of Readings*, Lewes: Falmer Press.

Scott, D. and Usher, R. (eds) (1996) *Understanding Educational Research*, London: Routledge.

Scott, D., Hurry, J., Hey, V. and Smith, M. (1997) *An Evaluation of the Accelerated Learning Programme*, London: London Institute of Education.

Simon, A. and Boyer, G. (1970a) *Mirrors for Behaviour*, Vol. 1, Philadelphia: Research for Better Schools.

Simon, A. and Boyer, G. (1974) *Mirrors for Behaviour*, Vol. 2, Philadelphia: Research for Better Schools.

Simon, A. and Boyer, G. (1970b) *Mirrors for Behaviour*, Vol. 3, Philadelphia: Research for Better Schools.

Simon, R. and Dippo, D. (1986) 'On Critical Ethnographic Work', *Anthropology and Education Quarterly*, 17(4): 195–202.

Simons, H. (1984) 'Negotiating Conditions for Independent Evaluations', in C. Adelman (ed.) *The Politics and Ethics of Evaluation*, London: Croom Helm.

Simons, H. (1988) *Getting to Know Schools in a Democracy: The Politics and Process of Evaluation*, Lewes: Falmer Press.

Smith, D. and Tomlinson, S. (1989) *The School Effect: A Study of Multiracial Comprehensives*, London: Policy Studies Institute.

Smith, L. and Keith, P. (1971) *Anatomy of an Educational Innovation*, New York: John Wiley.

Smith, N.L. (1982) 'The Context of Evaluation Practice in State Departments of Education', in N.L. Smith and D.N. Caulley (eds) *The Interaction of Evaluation and Policy: Case Reports from State Education Agencies*, Portland, Oregon: Northwest Regional Educational Laboratory (NREL), 159–78.

Solomon, R.L. (1949) 'An Extension of Control Group Design', *Psychological Bulletin*, 46: 137–50.

Stake, R. (ed.) (1975) *Evaluating the Arts in Education: A Responsive Approach*, Columbus, OH: Charles E. Merrill Publishing Company.

Stenhouse, L. (1975) *An Introduction to Curriculum Research and Development*, London: Heinemann.

Strauss, A. and Corbin, J. (1990) *Basics of Qualitative Research: Grounded Theory Procedures and Techniques*, London: Sage.

Strauss, A. and Corbin, J. (1994) 'Grounded Theory Methodology: An Overview', in N. Denzin and Y. Lincoln (eds) *Handbook of Qualitative Research*, London: Sage.

Stronach, I. and MacLure, M. (1997) *Educational Research Undone*, Buckingham: Open University Press.

Tyler, R. (1949) *Basic Principles of Curriculum and Instruction*, Chicago and London: The University of Chicago Press.

Underwood, J. and Underwood, G. (1995) *Integrated Learning Systems in UK Schools Final Report*, Leicester University School of Education, NCET.

Usher, R. (1993) 'Reflexivity', *Occasional Papers in Education and Interdisciplinary Studies, 3,* Southampton University, School of Education.

Usher, R. (1997) 'Telling a Story about Research and Research as Story-Telling: Postmodern Approaches to Social Research', in G. McKenzie, J. Powell and R. Usher (eds) *Understanding Social Research: Perspectives on Methodology and Practice*, London: Falmer Press.

Vygotsky, L.S. (1978) *Mind in Society*, Cambridge, Mass: MIT Press.

Walsh, P. (1993) *Education and Meaning: Philosophy in Practice*, London: Cassell.

Watson, L. (1976) 'Understanding a Life History as a Subjective Document: Hermeneutical and Phenomenological Perspectives', *Ethos, 4*: 95–131.

Weber, M. (1964) *The Theory of Social and Economic Organisation*, New York: Free Press.

Westkott, M. (1990) 'Feminist Criticism of the Social Sciences', in J. Nielsen (ed.) *Feminist Research Methods*, London: Westview Press.

Wilson, R. (1990) 'Sociology and the Mathematical Method', in A. Giddens and J. Turner (eds) *Social Theory Today*, London: Polity Press.

Winch, P. (1958) *The Idea of a Social Science and its Relation to Philosophy*, London: Routledge and Kegan Paul.

Winter, R. (1989) *Learning from Experience: Principles and Practice in Action Research*, Lewes: Falmer Press.

Wolf, R.L. (1974) 'The Use of Judicial Evaluation Methods in the Formation of Educational Policy', *Educational Evaluation and Policy Analysis*, 1: 19–28.

Wood, R. and Power, C. (1987) 'Aspects of the Competence–Performance Distinction: Educational, Psychological and Measurement Issues', *Journal of Curriculum Studies*, 19(5): 409–24.

Woods, P. and Sykes, P. (1987) 'The Use of Teacher Biographies in Professional

Self Development', in F. Todd (ed.) *Planning Continuing Professional Development,* London: Croom Helm.

Name Index

Subject Index